Open Bag

Open Bag

Memoir Of A Homeless PGA Tour Caddie

Pierre Van Achterbergh

Dedication

This book is dedicated to three very special people I had the honour and privilege of knowing and sharing special times with. Firstly to my brother Edwin, I want to say thanks for all your help and support dealing with all my problems. Then a thank you to Roger Morgan for being the true friend you always were. Last but not least thank you to Mark Mazo another true friend. Thank you guys and I apologise for being such a fool. I want to thank my golf buddies for their friendship and thank you to Robert Johnson for saving my sinking ship. Thanks also to my Durban buddy Martin Barnard who helped me a lot with all of this.

Pierre

If I wrote that Pierre was a great caddie I would be lying, although he could damn sure read a putt. One of the few that could send a golfer the wrong way on a dogleg par 4 and also convince his player to play a course with 10 out of 14 holes dog leg lefts while his player hits a fade. What I can say about Pierre is that he was a joy to spend time with both on and off the golf course. Whether it be having a Budweiser in the afternoon or having a Budweiser at night (not over dinner as food would take space away in his stomach for his Budweiser) or walking down the 72nd hole with a chance to win, he was always light and cheerful. The only time that I can recall him being down while in my presence was when I left my putt half an inch short on the last hole of Q-school to miss my card by a shot. That's how much it meant to him and how much he cared about me knowing how much it meant to me. Always a gentleman and one of the many great characters that has spent time on both the Nationwide and PGA Tours. A great friend that will always mean the world to me and my family.

R. Johnson PGA Tour Professional Golfer

Reflection

The biggest regret that I have to this day is not the fact that I shot myself in the foot and sank my ship of treasure due to my crazy irresponsible life and the stupid things I did, but the fact that I let my family down. For so long they supported me through the good and bad times especially my brother and one sister. My brother bailed me out countless times starting with my leaving America at the time. He funded many of my trips to Europe, always supporting me and he shared in the success I did have out on the Golf Tours. He helped me in my darkest times trying his best to get me on the straight and narrow. He got me into rehab for my gambling problem at the time and he really tried his utmost to help me find my way in life. Sadly the demons won the fight in the end and my family had no choice but to throw in the towel and wash their hands of me and my troubles. I guess in life there is only so much people can help if you don't want to help yourself, and that's what ended up happening to me. My family are all very firm family orientated folks, very successful and they could never understand or accept my wayward life and ways. This was the saddest part of everything as I lost all their support and respect along the way and I couldn't blame them, only myself. I caused such a rift between myself and my family that it could never be repaired and I became a total outcast in their books. This whole scenario could have played out so differently. However, the gambling demons stalked me all the way, finally winning and sending me to the gutters.

Prologue

Professional golf caddies live a very different life to most people. These guys travel around the world in a nomadic fashion living in hotels and spending their days walking around golf courses, working for and helping the best professional golfers in the world. They are a vital part of a two-man team that chase birdies and big money in a very lucrative world of professional golf. The golfer is the captain of the ship but the caddie is his right hand man, at the ready to provide useful information and clean up any mess the captain leaves behind. Apart from lugging a huge and heavy golf bag around, the duties of a professional golf caddie include many different things. First and foremost is knowing the different golf courses inside out. They must know the safest way from tee box to green avoiding all possible trouble. Whilst caddying, they must always have all the yardages from one point to the next at their fingertips. They must know what clubs are to be used for all the different shots and also when to make comments, either encouraging the golfer or warning them of any potential dangers that may be around the corner. Many times, a caddie can be faced with a situation whereby they disagree with a player. These situations always get the heart beating as the last thing you want to do is give your man a bad call, losing lots of money in the process. These guys in many ways, live both a very challenging and exciting life at the same time. Flying all over the world earning big money and hoping to be in the mix every week once the tournaments finish. There are some serious amounts of money to be won in the world of professional golf.

An easy way to really sum up the life of a caddie that travels and works on the different golf tours, is like rolling the dice in a casino. One never knows what is going to happen from one week to the next. Being a professional caddie your fate is mostly out of your control as everything really depends on how the golfer is going to perform. So it's all like riding a fast rollercoaster. Sometimes you fall out and other times you make it to the end.

In this business there will always be two sides to the whole story. There are the struggling caddies, living week to week hoping and praying for a success and a result on the golf course. This could mean just making it to the weekend and having a bonus of some sort. Then you have the caddies riding the gravy train, working for great golfers and these guys are just printing money and cashing in week after week. All the caddies are in fact doing the exact same job. I guess some are just better at it than others. As far as I am concerned, in this business luck has a lot to do with things. I have seen caddies without work, pick up a bag in the parking lot before a tournament and then go on to win. That's being in the right place at the right time for sure. Others struggle week-to-week working really hard but have no real results to show for their efforts. Some caddies on the Tours have always struggled, never having hooking up with a good golfer and as a result have got nowhere. Others appear on the scene and before you knew it they win tournaments and find themselves in the big time and are making big money. I have seen great caddies struggle and I have seen shit caddies go all the way to the top. I always said a bad jockey can win on a good horse but a good jockey will never win on a bad horse. This applies to golf for sure, with silly and strange things happening all the time. As I have already mentioned, for most of the caddies it was all just like a roll of the dice.

Off the golf course these guys know how to party. They constantly live it up, spending their nights eating in expensive restaurants and hanging out in pubs and bars, in different cities all over the world. Some are more conservative and choose to live a more relaxed life on the road. Though in general, it's golf during the day and good food and booze at night. Many spend late nights in strip clubs, nightclubs and casino's, waking the next morning with a sore head, though they all get used to this after a while. In many respects, it could all really be described as a travelling circus of sorts. These guys all hang on to the good golfers they work for, whilst the others are always on the lookout for the next Tiger Woods to come along.

How people become professional caddies is a question asked a thousand times and there is no real or valid answer. There is no set rule or system to follow and each caddie will tell a very different story. Some start out as a progression from their work at country clubs caddying for members, others work for a friend who is a professional golfer, some are related to the golfer, but most are guys who love to travel and party whilst knowing this game inside out.

When things were going well during the tournaments, all was good between the golfer and the caddie. However, when things went wrong often the caddie took the blame, in most cases this ended up with them getting fired. For this reason, some caddies stayed with the same golfer for years and others bounced around between bags, in hope of finding a great golfer to build a good relationship with. All in all, it is a performance-based job, certainly for the golfer but this also applies to the caddie.

Something people may not be aware of is the fact that most professional caddies somehow earned a nickname on the golf tour. They usually earned these nicknames as a result of something they had done whilst working. The nicknames always stuck and even after years working on the different golf tours, people only knew them by their nicknames, not having a clue what their real name actually is.

During my years on the professional golf tours I travelled many windy and twisty roads. I worked on just about every golf tour in the world. Starting on the Web.com Tour in America, which is believed to be the training ground for up and coming golfers, and the stepping-stone to the big money, the main PGA Tour. Here you had guys, both golfers and caddies, with dreams of making the big time, travelling all over America playing tournaments in small towns or big cities, chasing birdies and a life of luxury. Some saw these dreams come true and others saw their dreams go up in smoke. It was an exciting world of travelling, expectations, highs and lows. Many of the caddies were guys that loved golf; many had left good jobs in order to try their luck on the links. Here they would hope to find the next star in the making. Caddies would come and go as some would go back to real jobs, not making it in the golfing world. Others ended up in the big time, making the big money on the main PGA Tour. It was all really a hit and miss business and this applied to the golfers as well. For me being a gambler needing constant excitement, it was a perfect fit. I always said in this game it was chicken one day and feathers the next. That is the perfect way to describe this world of professional golf.

Once my breakthrough finally came to the main PGA Tour it was a different world of glitz, glamour and huge money. Cream rises to the top and usually only the very best golfers and caddies stay on this stage. Here it was the huge crowds, the television cameras constantly nearby, that really made the PGA Tour a fantasy world of sorts. Out here it was pressure packed tournaments every week, with every putt having a huge amount of money riding on it. Over in Europe you had the same thing with guys trying to hit the big time, starting on the Challenge Tour travelling all over Europe, dreaming of playing on the European Tour. It's the same story for all the caddies once they succeed in reaching their respective main tour; the Big Time and the Big Money. The main difference between the PGA Tour and the European Tour was the travelling. The tournaments on the European Tour are played all over the world in many different countries. This would mean some big trips between tournaments, sometimes having to fly thousands of miles Sunday evening in order to get ready for the next event the following day. On the PGA Tour, many of the tournaments were close enough to drive to. Many caddies would travel together if one of them had a car as this would really help keep the travel costs down.

In due course I also came to work on the Ladies European Tour, which was also a world of its own. For a guy going from the men's tour, playing the biggest tournaments in the world to the Ladies European Tour, the feeling I had could be best described as, falling of a ladder. Things were just so much more low key, and not nearly as exciting as the men's tour. An easy way to describe it was the Oomphh was just missing out there. It was all very girlie stuff and after watching the power golf on the men's tour, it was like watching a dead fish trying to swim. Walking along the golf courses the conversations were totally different, and I thought the guys that were caddying on this tour were guys who couldn't crack it in the men's world. I thought they were settling for second best. For me anyway, after the heights I had reached in golf before it was soul destroying being relegated to this tour. For me it was very sad when I thought about it. I only had myself to blame. However, one good thing did come from this tour, there were some pretty girls and nice legs to look at.

Then I spent time on the Asian Tour. This was also a different kettle of fish. The big plus here was visiting many exotic destinations. Sadly, the money wasn't really as big and the competition was a lot weaker. Often it would be hard work, walking some long golf courses in some very hot temperatures that you'd expect in certain parts of Asia. In general it was cheap to get around and for me there were beautiful and sexy girls everywhere. This tour is growing however, and the golfing world is seeing more and more very good players coming through from here.

In Africa the Sunshine Tour caters to the local golfers with black caddies usually on the bags. The prize money is relatively small too and only when the European Tour goes to Africa things change. The European Tour has a few tournaments co-sanctioned with the Sunshine Tour and the prize money is really good. As a result of this, a lot of good European golfers make the trip to Africa in hope of picking up a good cheque, whilst also playing on the great golf courses it has to offer.

So in a nutshell, one has all these different golf tours each with its own purpose and level of importance. The one thing they all have in common is that everybody on any tour, is chasing their dream to hit the big time in golf. It's a bunch of characters riding a non-stop roller coaster of birdies, bogies and big money around the world.

As for the "Big Time", well that is perfectly embodied by our four Majors. People have conflicting ideas on which is the most important major in the world. Some say the Masters, others claim it's the British Open, others say the US Open. However you cut the cake, these majors are the icing. These are the tournaments every single professional golfer and caddie has dreamt about since childhood.

In my travels on the golf tours I was very blessed and fortunate to have caddied in some of these major tournaments. Being a part of any of these majors is a very, very, special privilege. Here you get to hang out and work with only the very best in the game, being close and upfront. I have to believe any golfer has reached the pinnacle of this sport when they can say they have played in a major tournament.

When one looks at what Jack Nicklaus and Tiger Woods have accomplished in the majors it is mind boggling to say the least. Most golfers and caddies are lucky to win one major in their careers, and would give their left arm to do so. Most professional golfers play for years without coming close to playing in a major, let alone winning one. I can assure you that being between the ropes at any one of the majors is an experience one can only describe as magical. Arriving at one of these tournaments there is a real buzz around the town and a special vibe lingers in the air. The whole town that these tournaments are played in, perhaps the whole country, are focused on every little thing happening that week of the year. There are the TV crews, news reporters, thousands of people spectating and only a very small and select group of caddies and golfers. During any one of these weeks accommodation is almost impossible to find and very expensive. The city or town is a mad house and very busy. I guess when you find yourself at one of the majors you have reached the top of the ladder. Once the week gets going things become crazy and hectic, with thousands of people turning up even on the practice days. At night the pubs and restaurants are packed to the rafters and its golf talk everywhere you go. Once the tournament gets going things become a lot more serious and inside the ropes it all becomes one huge pressure cooker, with each shot representing huge money and fame. There you are working with the best golfers in the world but believe me, it is all extremely tense and serious. Every birdie or bogey is big out there and the caddies have to be on their toes at all times. Making the cut is goal number one and then moving up the leaderboard becomes the main focus.

I can clearly remember arriving at Carnoustie in Scotland for the Open, my first major as a caddie. There I was on the Tuesday, in the locker room and of all people I happened to sit down next to was Tiger Woods. It sounds stupid but I was overawed by the man and just sat there watching him put his golf shoes on. "How the fuck did I ever arrive here" I remember thinking to myself, realizing there I was amongst the best in the world. As I have mentioned before being between the ropes was tense and exciting but also a little scary. This was golf at its best and a real pleasure to witness. Sadly my first major didn't last too long as Steve Alker, the professional I was working for missed the cut. We played our practice round with Adam Scott and he was a pleasure to be around, hitting fairway after fairway and green after green, he was immense. At the same time he was also a true gentleman and offered us advice whenever he saw fit to.

Apart from the golf I also got to meet and hang out with some of the top caddies and believe me, some of these guys have made an absolute fortune in this business. Away from the golf course people everywhere wanted to chat to you and in a little way, you were also a celebrity of sorts that week. I could only imagine the fanfare and experience of actually winning a major tournament, and how fortunate those guys were that managed to achieve this feat. When I worked for Pablo Larrazabal and we arrived at my next major, the Open at Royal Birkdale, it was all a little different. Here I was working for one of the hottest and most promising players on the European tour. We had won the French Open so this kid was big news and in the frontline. Everywhere we went we had crowds following us looking for autographs and it was all crazy. I also had a fat bank account at the time and I was riding the crest of a wave. At this time I was in an elite group of successful professional caddies. On Friday we made the cut having played in some very windy bad weather. I then got to caddie on the weekend, really experiencing the magic of a major golf tournament. During the week I met a pretty English girl who was very impressed that I worked for a top golfer, she worked in one of the local pubs and we actually ended up dating for a while after that.

So to put it all in a nutshell being part of any major golf tournament is an honour and a privilege. It is safe to say that only a handful of people get to experience all of this and I bet a very large amount of the golfing population would love to do so. I worked extremely hard to get to the majors but will always feel I am very fortunate to have had this opportunity. I will always be grateful for having the opportunity to be part of the Majors and the memories will accompany me for the remainder of my days.

In all the years I travelled around the world chasing the birdies and dollars I worked for a lot of different golfers. Most were nice guys who treated me well and then there were the few arseholes that appear from time to time throughout my account. Of all the golfers I caddied for I have to say Richard Johnson was the biggest gentleman and by far the best guy I ever caddied for. Apart from working for him we were close friends both on and off the course. I travelled across America with him and his family and I spent time at his house in Augusta Georgia in the off weeks. The cool thing was that Richard was always keen to play some golf with us caddies and that was always a treat for us. Many of the golfers stayed away from us caddies and lived the high life, Richard was very down to earth and we loved it. I thought this guy could have been a world-beater. He had won many tournaments on the Web.com Tour in America. When he finally got into the big time on the PGA Tour for some crazy reason he couldn't get going and this will always remain a mystery to me.

Apart from being mates with Richard I also became buddies with his two brothers Rob and Geoff. Rob at the time was a young good looking guy that the girls loved, and on his trips to America from Wales where he lived, he always had the girls at his feet. His brother Geoff was a party guy who could drink with the best of them, so when these guys came to America it was always party time. They were also good golfers and I managed to play some golf with them too. Their dad Peter was a well-respected golf instructor in Wales and a great guy, so these guys all grew up around golf. When you worked for guys like Richard Johnson this was the greatest job in the world as out on the golf course you could have fun whether things were going well or bad. There was no club throwing or tantrums and that's how I've always believed things should.

The day I sent him into the shit at Poppy Hills on the 14th hole during the big PGA Tournament he went nuts, but who could blame him. Yet here once again he demonstrated what a gentleman he was by not firing me. I can promise you every other golfer in this world would have fired their caddie if this had happened to them. So in this business it was always a privilege and honour to work for the really nice guys but no fun at all working for the hotheads and arsehole golfers.

The day I stood on that 14th tee box at Poppy Hills golf course during a big PGA Tour tournament in America, the professional golf caddies worst nightmare came true. Richard had fallen sick that week and as a result he did not play the practice rounds as these guys normally did.

This tournament was played on three different golf courses, so it was up to me to find the time and plan how we would navigate them. I had to check all the yardages and make note of any dangers that lay ahead of us, so that I could guide him around if he was well enough to play once the tournament started. Having very limited time and three golf courses to figure out I decided on a short cut that was to backfire and cost many thousands of dollars in the end. I found a golf cart and proceeded to drive around all the golf courses thinking I could do things the easy way.

As things finally unfolded a sick Richard Johnson got out of bed to play golf and amazingly, right from the first day shot to the top of the leaderboard. By the time we arrived at the 14th hole at Poppy Hills, against all the odds, we were tied for the lead playing against the best golfers in the world including Tiger Woods and Sergio Garcia. Standing on this tee box I suddenly got a knot in my stomach as I realised that I had no clue how to play this hole. Somehow driving around in the golf cart I had missed the hole completely, and now I found myself in deep shit.

Looking at me Richard said, "So what is the play here?" and with my heart in my throat, I had to come up with a reply and fast.

I knew this was going to be a 50/50 guess so I replied, "It's a dog leg to the right". I suggested he hit the three wood and pointed at a tall dry tree in the distance as the target, as luck had it, the yardage book couldn't help me either.

Smashing this shot straight at the tall dry tree he said, "That should be good hey?"

I stood there actually praying that I had guessed correctly and that I could bullshit my way out of this serious predicament I found myself in. Leaving the tee box I walked towards the tall dry tree, my mouth so dry I couldn't swallow.

The next thing, all hell broke loose and shouting at the top of his voice Richard Johnson said, "What the fuck man, this hole is a dogleg to the left you arsehole."

Turning around I then realized that I had sent him in the totally wrong direction and his ball was lying in amongst thick trees virtually unplayable. I could never really describe the feeling that washed over me and standing there I looked a total idiot with a large crowd following to add to my embarrassment and despair.

"How the hell did I ever let this happen," kept racing through my mind.

*   *   *

As a reader I will lead you through this crazy and exciting journey across the world from nowhere, to the very top in the world of professional golf. I'm sure most guys can only dream of doing anything like this, and one would think once you have reached the top of the mountain like I did, you would do anything to stay there. But no, I jumped off the mountain top with no parachute, crashing and burning, landing up in a nightmare situation that was unbelievable. Once I hit rock bottom and found myself on the streets, the reality of everything kicked in when I ended up living with homeless people who had no shoes and nothing to eat. Landing up firstly on a farm near Pretoria with some rough types from the other side of the tracks. I spent my days in a hot dirty kitchen cooking for over 300 homeless people. I also got to realise in South Africa since the New Government, many white people found themselves unemployed and homeless. The shoe was on the other foot now Government wise. When I ended up in this situation I found myself in, it was hard not hard to think of pulling the plug with life. The days I spent here were a living nightmare, living amongst down and out people with my pride in shreds living on hand outs.

When I finally couldn't take anymore I hit the streets and going to Durban I found myself back in the same boat amongst the homeless people. Here, as the weather is the warmest both summer and winter, you find many destitute people, they could at least shower on the beach under cold water and sleep outdoors. The homeless shelters here are a mess and really dirty places, with some extremely bad people living there. Drunks and drug addicts, you name it these people are there and there I was slap bang in the middle of it all.

When you end up like this and think back to the five star hotels and high life it makes everything so much harder to digest and deal with. South Africa has a very high rate of unemployment and as I say, many white people can't find any employment. Local charities try to feed the homeless at times but there is never enough food and too many mouths. Here you had many people sleeping in one room with some of the people not having bathed in days or washed their clothes for weeks. It was black and white mixed. I pictured Hell in the Bible and it had to be very much like this.

I spent time in these places and knew it was all self-inflicted and I had only myself to blame.

One

I guess having been born into a crazy and very dysfunctional home could have had something to do with the crazy way my life finally turned out. My father, already in his late forties, had married my mother who was only seventeen and I was born just after her eighteenth birthday. To add to this crazy situation my mother was wife number four, so it's not difficult to figure out that this was all a recipe destined for disaster.

My father was a wealthy property developer at the time but he spent more time at the golf club than he did either at his office, or at home. This guy honestly spent every day of his life at the golf club, working a few hours in the morning at his office and the rest of the day at the golf club, drinking, playing golf and cards with friends for money. This all caused constant friction at home as my father stayed at the golf club until late most nights, drinking with his buddies once they'd finished playing golf. I guess as my mother was a lot younger than my father she felt insecure and neglected. Come the weekends it was the same old story but a happy time for me as my father often took me along to the golf club with him. The funny thing was, he was never really a great golfer as he played to a handicap of 12, but you couldn't drag this guy away from the golf course for love nor money. I suppose it was more about socialising with his buddies, and driving home it was a slow and careful process after all the drinks. This all led to bad vibes back home and numerous arguments. My mother and father both played tennis too. On the odd weekend my father would make an effort to go to the tennis club with my mother to try and keep the peace. I am not really sure why, but since a very young age I never clicked with my mother, as I always preferred to be around my father. The times he did actually spend at home, he loved to entertain as we lived in a huge house with a swimming pool and tennis court. My mother got pretty involved with the cocktails during these parties and once all the people had left the arguments started. As a kid lying in bed at night listening to all this it was very upsetting to say the least. I guess to try and make up for his shortcomings my father spoiled my mother, buying her expensive gifts and taking her for weekends away. However, everything went up in smoke when finally the dam wall burst, as my mother couldn't deal with all the late nights my father spent drinking with his golf buddies, she decided to divorce him. The divorce was bitter and it was all a pretty traumatic period of my childhood. My mother, now with three kids to raise, moved to a town called Bloemfontein. I wanted to stay with my father but had no option as I had to go with my mother. I was very upset at this turn of events, as I loved going to the golf club with my dad. My mother on the other hand hated everything related to golf as according to her, it had ruined her marriage. I'm not really too sure but I do think the instability I suffered most of my life stemmed from all of this, but who really knows.

So my mother and three kids left Johannesburg and from here onwards my mother and I had a very rocky and unstable relationship. She was always telling us what a bad and irresponsible man my father was and sadly she also developed a drinking problem, I guess due to the stress of the divorce. This problem would follow her for the rest of her life and although she would argue fiercely that she wasn't an alcoholic, sadly it was clear to us she was.

Despite this she was actually a very beautiful woman and she turned heads wherever she went with her long blonde hair. Before the divorce my father had bought her a flashy and expensive sports car so this, plus her good looks drew much male attention once we arrived in Bloemfontein. It wasn't long before my mother started dating a man from a prominent Bloemfontein family and now she was the queen bee in her new environment.

I was sent to Grey College, one of South Africa's top schools but things at home were always unpleasant for me and we were not allowed to see my father much. So from the get go I developed a very rebellious streak and this followed me during all of my schooling days. Once my mother married this new man we left Bloemfontein and moved again, causing more instability in my life once more.

This guy turned out to be a really good man but the bad vibes between my mother and I only got worse and her drinking got worse too.

My mother and stepfather then bought a small country hotel in a small town called Ixopo, the town Alan Paton describes in the opening lines of "Cry, The Beloved Country": "There is a lovely road which runs from Ixopo into the hills. These hills are grass covered and rolling, and they are lovely beyond any singing of it." Published in 1948, the year in which apartheid later became law, Paton's novel was a social protest against the structures of society at that time. Reflecting many years later, this literary backdrop seems to have provided a dark sense of foreboding for the violent conflict I would come to experience with black native workers also seeking wealthy Tour players for whom to caddie.

At Ixopo, a little under 150 km west of Durban, I was sent to the boarding house. This was crazy as my parents owned this hotel in town and the school was only three kilometres away at the most, yet I was stuck in a boarding house. I could never get over this and as a result, my rebelliousness only got worse.

One Saturday the school swimming team were going to a swimming gala and being the good swimmer I was from the years of practise in my father's pool in our old house, I was selected as part of the team. My best buddy and I then devised a plan to have some fun during the ride on the school bus. From my parent's liquor store at the hotel, I stole a bottle of vodka and mixing this with Coca-Cola we smuggled it on to the school bus. By the time we arrived at the swimming gala we were so drunk we couldn't swim and we all thought it was so funny. The following Monday I was seated in the headmaster's office along with my parents and they were informed that I was getting expelled from the school. My mother went nuts to say the least.

After this, things between my mother and I hit a rock bottom and my stepfather finally used his important connections back in Bloemfontein to get me back into Grey College. For a pupil expelled from a small country school this was a major deal for my stepfather to organize, but somehow he managed to do it. Grey College is one of the top schools in South Africa so this was basically a miracle. So I was sent packing to boarding school in Bloemfontein, a further 600 km west, and from then on I was pretty much on my own in life.

Arriving at the school and being sent to the boarding house I hated everything right from the get go. Everything was very strict and old fashioned, run by real staunch Afrikaans teachers; it reminded me of how I envisioned jail when I was a child. The other pupils all seemed to come from strict and religious homes; mostly Afrikaans kids and I definitely did not fit into this picture at all. I was not a happy camper as by then I was already smoking and bunking out of school, heading to parties and drinking on regular occasions. At Grey College, this was a very serious offence. This concentration camp vibe led me getting into all sorts of trouble. Back in those days you were marched into the headmaster's office and bending over you got your arse whipped with a cane. I was in and out of this office on a regular basis and getting caught one night sneaking out I got six of the best and could not sit on my arse for days. At this school rugby was the big thing and Grey College year after year had the best team in the country. I did play a little rugby for the fourth team but actually did very well in athletics. On the academic side of things I was hopeless, always failing the exams that we had to sit. Generally, I was a really bad scholar. To put things in a nutshell my schooling days were a total disaster and I definitely was not a kid any parent could be proud of.

My parents were hoping I would become a good scholar at this great school but I chose another path. I discovered girls and soon I could be seen sneaking out of the boarding house at night to go visit them around town.

During my time here I had not seen much of my real father in Johannesburg, I knew he had married his fifth wife, also a lot younger than himself but this was no surprise to me.

Two

I somehow eventually managed to scrape through and finish school. As these were the days of apartheid in South Africa, I then had to take part in compulsory military training.

I found myself in the South African Navy in Cape Town and for me the good life started. Now I could party and chase girls and being a navy boy certainly helped the cause. Here it was all a carefree life and one Sunday at a nudist beach called Sandy Bay, I met a forty two year old, extremely good looking single woman. I was only nineteen at the time so this mature lady knocked me off my feet. She had a fancy apartment in Sea Point and for the next year she taught me all the tricks a young man needed to know.

I remember taking her home to meet my parents at Christmas time. My mother was horrified and as asked us to leave.

I moved around during my navy days and leaving Cape Town I spent time in Durban and finally finished up in Pretoria. After leaving this older women I had developed all the tools needed to charm the ladies and it had been a great learning curve.

Finally leaving the navy I decided to work in the hotel industry as I had learnt some things from helping in my parent's hotel. Moving to Durban I found a position as a trainee manager and now new doors opened up to me. In the hotel they had a bar and dance club called "The Rainbow Club". Here you could pick and choose between all the pretty girls you could imagine.

Life was good and I was learning the hotel trade and it wasn't long before I found a better position as an assistant manager in one of the big beachfront hotels in Durban. This was a big step up in life. Come holiday season the hotel was packed with guests from all over the world and being the assistant manager I had some clout. When I wasn't working the beach was only a stone throw away. I enjoyed spending my time off here despite the long hours I had to work. Whilst here, one of my colleagues that I'd become friends with introduced me to his cousin, a pretty girl call Sarah. I then met her best friend, a stunning blonde girl called Chantal and this is where things started to get messy.

When people say lightning cannot strike twice in the same place, I have to beg to differ as during this time the craziest shit happened. One night Sarah informed me that she was pregnant and I was responsible. She then told me that her mother was sending her to England to have an abortion. I obviously had no say in the matter and once Sarah had left I started dating her best friend Chantal.

Then as I said, the lightning struck again and very soon Chantal was breaking the news to me that in fact, she was also pregnant. Hearing this I knew big trouble was around the corner as her dad did not like me in the slightest, and she was his blue-eyed baby girl. To make things worse she was only seventeen years old and I knew major shit was going to hit the fan. Her parents also knew about her friend Sarah by now, so how could the shit not hit the fan?

Once her mother had heard the whole story she took me to one side and in a very serious voice said, "Believe me, her dad is going to shoot you. I'm not joking, you must pack your bags and leave town as soon as possible. I will look after Chantal but you have to leave. This could end in a serious tragedy my boy."

Knowing the mother I realised she was being honest and she was right, the dad would shoot me, as he was that kind of guy.

A week later I found myself in Johannesburg jobless, knocking on my father's door. Having not seen much of my father over the years it was at least good to see him. Soon I was hanging out with him at the golf club most days, which reminded me of my earlier childhood. I had played a little golf before but now he taught me properly and within three months I was a respectable golfer with a handicap of 12, just like him. I fell in love with the game and hit balls until my hands were covered in blisters.

In the meanwhile I found a job as a sales rep. I was given a company car so I was up and running once again. Back in Durban Chantal told me I had left just in time, as her dad had gone mad threatening to kill me. We were both far too young to consider marriage so it was decided sadly that we were never going to see each other again. As difficult as this was, it was the sensible thing to do under the circumstances.

The lady my dad had married was young and good looking; she hooked me up with her friends so I was having no problems at all on the social front. Life simply revolved around working, the golf club and partying.

Over the next couple of years I'd changed jobs and girlfriends a few times but had also developed a pretty serious gambling problem. This all started with a golfing trip to Sun City where I discovered the casino. The game roulette had me by the balls from the get go and little did I know this game would eventually haunt and cripple me for the rest of my life. At first it was all fun and games but it slowly progressed into a life changing problem.

A few years later I had lost contact with Chantal but I knew she had given birth to a baby girl. That all seemed to belong to another life by then. The strange thing was that whilst I would move back to Durban several times in coming years, I would never see Chantal again.

Three

Moving nearer to Durban I got a Sales Rep job with a big food company and the north coast was my area to service and operate in. In a town called Vryheid 300km north of Durban, the company had a depot, which I was in charge of, and it was here I discovered a restaurant that was struggling financially. The many evenings I went to eat at this restaurant I had got to know the owners quite well. However, the talk in town was that the restaurant was going downhill big time. One evening whilst visiting the restaurant, I spoke to the owners and I made them an offer to buy the place. I did not have much money due to my irresponsible gambling but I could at least offer them a down payment, and pay the balance in monthly instalments.

Before I really knew it I was the owner of a struggling restaurant and I decided to change everything and turn it into a steakhouse called "The Stetson Grill". As I had no cash it all had to be done on a shoe string budget. I went to the local wood mill and bought lots of rough timber cheaply. I then panelled the whole place out in this rough wood creating an old Texas feel. So there I had it, my very own restaurant and I'd managed to finish it for next to nothing. I managed to make the place look like an old Texas steakhouse of sorts and The Stetson Grill opened in Vryheid.

I knew the catering and food industry fairly well, so I had a simple menu offering great steaks and all sorts of huge burgers with different toppings. Once the restaurant had opened it was jam packed most nights. The place itself wasn't really that big and could only seat about 50 people, so some nights it was like a railway station with people constantly coming and going. Having the connections to all the butcheries in town due to my real job as a sales rep, we served only the best steaks at a great price and the Stetson Grill became the talk of the town. We kept the menu pretty simple but if it was a good steak you wanted the Stetson Grill was the place. One night two guys arrived at the restaurant and ordering food they requested a bottle of wine. Having no license to sell alcohol I supplied them with a bottle from our private stock out the back. When they paid the bill I added the wine as a desert as I did for a few of our regular customers. The next fucking thing I knew these guys arrested me, they were undercover cops and I had no idea. I later learnt that the owner of another restaurant had sent them there. I ended up spending the night in jail and later appeared in court and was forced to pay a huge fine. So I guess in this town we were loved by many but hated by some. There were times I could not believe that this whole thing had actually worked out for me; never had I dreamt it would become so successful. It was all done pretty much on the spur of the moment and on a whim initially.

I still had my Sales Rep job so I employed a manager to work for me. The Stetson Grill started making waves in town once again. With the good cash flow steadily coming from the restaurant I started to visit The Wild Coast Casino on a regular basis, losing big amounts of money. It was easy come easy go as far as I was concerned. Stupidly, I thought of myself as Mister Big Spender.

Due to the large amounts of money I had to throw around I got the VIP treatment at the Wild Coast Casino, always getting complimentary accommodation and drinks on the house. Once I entered the casino it was always that exciting and electric feeling in the air that captivated me. Once I hit the roulette table I was in another world and glued to my chair. Roulette was the one game that seemed to provide an adrenalin rush and this, mixed with many cocktails made me lose contact with reality. As casinos have no windows or clocks it is really easy to lose track of time. Quite often I would leave the casino, having been in there so long the sun had set and risen again. The Wild Coast

Casino is situated on the south coast and it's a really beautiful part of South Africa. Leaving here I was always depressed and angry, as I knew how irresponsible I was throwing big amounts of money away.

Sadly, I finally let things spiral totally out of control and before I knew it both my job and The Stetson Grill were swept out from under my feet. I had finally gambled the whole fucking lot away. Broke as a church mouse I finally had no choice, I went back to Johannesburg, tail between my legs.

Back hanging out with my dad once more, I gambled on the golf course making enough money to survive for a while and I was basically a ship with no sails, just floating around it seemed. For some crazy reason, I knew deep down inside I was a drifter of sorts and the real world and responsibility of it was not for me. Little did I know then, sooner or later I would discover a world I finally belonged in but that was all down the road.

I bounced around for some time between jobs, partying hard and drinking the nights away and it always seemed that I was on the road to nowhere. People around me were getting married, buying houses, working their way up in life but none of this appealed to me, I knew that much.

During all of this I had met a young waitress at one of the pubs I used to hang out in. Sure as shit the lightning struck once again as she fell pregnant only weeks later. I found myself in the same old boat again. I couldn't get over how stupid and irresponsible I had been. I knew marriage was never going to be on the cards for me in this lifetime so telling her this she decided to go her own way.

Four

The next major chapter in my life opened when I left Johannesburg and moved to a town called Pietersburg. Here I was offered another job as a Sales Rep. Shortly after moving I joined the local golf club. Here I made some good friends and all my time was spent either working or hanging out at the golf club playing golf or socializing.

One Saturday whilst at the club I met a huge guy called Kallie who was great fun and we had a game of golf together. From the moment I met Kallie we got along like a house on fire. Having a few beers afterwards we chatted and he said that he lived in a big house by himself that he was renting from somebody. By the time I left the golf club that evening, we had arranged that I was going to rent a room from him, and before I knew it, there I was living with this guy that I'd only just met. Kallie and I spent a lot of time together and became really good buddies.

My new buddy Kallie was a popular guy in town and having so many friends meant there was always something going on at his house. As South Africans love to braai and entertain there were many get togethers with guys from all over town, especially the golf club pitching up. The house was huge and having a live in maid, we lived like kings. Kallie was really a big guy and one incident I thought was going to put me in hospital. Kallie had a pretty redhead girlfriend who always hung out at the house. One week Kallie went out of town for a few days so his girlfriend and I spent time together drinking and talking. I'm not exactly sure how it all happened but I ended up in bed with his girlfriend one night. The next morning I started to panic, not sure what I was going to do about this. By the time Kallie returned I was a nervous wreck and whilst we were hanging out at the golf club, I finally decided to tell him the story.

Expecting the absolute worst I nearly fell off my chair when Kallie calmly replied "She is a great in bed don't you think."

I was gob smacked as Kallie actually laughed telling me that he just kept her around as she was great in bed. So as it happened we were just two bachelors living the good life in a huge house, having fun, playing a lot of golf and partying.

One day during a round of golf Kallie said, "Hey, what do you think of playing rugby in America?"

I wasn't sure what he was on about but he explained to me that rugby was becoming more popular in America. Some rugby clubs paid good money to players to go and play for them, plus the airfare to get there. Looking at Kallie who stood tall and hefty I could see he was the rugby type for sure.

"Have you played rugby?" he asked.

I had played for the fourth team back at Grey College so I replied, "Yes, but not that good my man."

Kallie then told me that he was thinking of going to play rugby in America as he had been made an offer by a rugby team in Kansas. I knew I was out of the picture as a little school rugby was one thing, but this was a different ball game he was talking about.

Over the next few weeks Kallie got more serious about the rugby thing and finally he had it all set up saying, "Well buddy, I'm on my way to Kansas to play rugby." This left me looking for accommodation as my comfortable stay in the big house was going to be all over.

Once he had left I moved into a small apartment and my boring life carried on as usual. It was maybe a few months later that I met a guy called Stefan whilst having a drink. We got talking and he told me that he was going to America on holiday. Hearing this I told him about my friend Kallie and the rugby story.

"That sounds pretty cool," he said. "Maybe I can go and visit this Kallie guy."

Over the next few weeks I got to know Stefan pretty well and he suggested that I join him on his holiday to America. Hearing this I laughed saying, "Shit buddy are you nuts? Going to the States is fucking expensive in case you don't know, especially considering the bad exchange rate."

There was no way I could entertain this thought, Stefan started laughing at me and replied, "Man, you only live once my bro."

My life in South Africa had been full of ups and downs and was going nowhere, so the thought of travelling was exciting to me, but financially it was totally out of the question.

One night having a few drinks, Stefan said, "How about I buy your ticket and you can pay me back sometime?"

Looking back things were a bit of a blur after that discussion with Stefan, I didn't need asking twice. Once I knew that I had the opportunity to go to America, getting all the paper work sorted became a huge pain in the arse. In South Africa dealing with this seemed to take an eternity. My first visit to the American embassy took hours and at some stage I honestly wondered if it was all worth the trouble. Dealing with the Home Affairs Office was another huge pain in the arse. I had spent countless hours running around organizing everything. My passport, my visa, and all the paperwork I needed for my trip were now in place. Somehow I seemed to be on my way to America. I guess all this was done on nervous energy, as I wasn't too sure what lay around the next corner. One thing I did know was that I was embarking on an adventure that will never be forgotten.

The original plan was a visit to New York and then locate Kallie in Kansas. We thought a trip to Las Vegas could also be on the cards at some stage. This was obviously an exciting prospect being the gambler that I was. All in all we had a three-week window to work with. I cashed all the money I had into dollars, which got me nearly $1300. I was also in debt to Stefan for the ticket but what the hell; I was off to America, the land of the free and the brave.

Five

The day finally came and we were leaving South Africa. The huge jumbo jet took off and I looked out of the little window watching the ground vanish beneath us. Little did I know it would be many years before I ever saw South Africa again.

During the flight we consumed our fair share of cocktails, passing out more than falling asleep. However, I was in for a huge surprise as we approached New York. Down below us I saw huge building's, which looked like they were rising up to meet us. It looked like one huge concrete jungle down there.

Waking my buddy Stefan up I said, "Hey look at this shit," and leaning over me he sat there, eyes wide open and almost speechless.

"What the fuck?" was about all I could hear him uttering, straining to peer out of the window.

For two guys from Africa it all looked like another planet down there. Once we exited the airport we really got to experience the madness, with everything moving at a hundred miles per hour.

"Fuck, is every car here yellow or what?" Stefan said.

Laughing I replied, "No shit buddy."

Finally catching a taxi we headed for Manhattan, this was apparently the place to hang out in New York for a good time. Driving along we were both amazed by this crazy city, huge buildings, lights and non-stop traffic, it really was like a concrete jungle.

In Manhattan we soon discovered our money wasn't going to last very long as accommodation was really expensive. We also realized that this city had a pulse and vibe all of its own. In a sports bar we got to drink Budweiser, the famous American beer and we watched American sport, which we didn't know much about. Watching the passing parade outside was also fascinating. Here the people were like ants running around non-stop. For a few days we did all of the things that regular tourists do, checking out Central Park, China Town, the Statue of Liberty and it was all a great experience.

We also discovered that the ladies loved our accents for some reason and people wanted to talk to us everywhere we went. I remember Stefan laughing as he said, "This is the American Dream, you open your mouth and the ladies panties drop. How good is that!"

It was funny but in reality, actually the truth.

New York was a blast and we were sorry to leave but the money situation finally forced us onwards. Leaving New York we headed for Kansas City. By this time I had located Kallie and we were on our way to see him. The journey was a long one, but definitely worth it. Arriving in Kansas City we burst out laughing when we finally found Kallie. There he stood facing us wearing cowboy boots and a cowboy hat.

"Howdy y'all," he joked when he saw us; it really was great seeing him again.

"This is how everybody looks in Texas," he explained. I couldn't believe that people actually wore clothes like this, especially him.

Kallie had bought a cheap conversion van and the three of us climbed into it. It was really cool with a huge swivelling captain's chairs and a great music system. He then explained to us that he was living in the university town of Lawrence, located just outside of Kansas City and he was playing rugby for the local team. He told us Lawrence was a small party town full of students and they loved to have a good time. We asked what he meant. "Oh man, the girls lie on their backs when I talk," Kallie joked. "Ha, the accent? You're telling me!" I replied.

With music blaring we hit the road and driving along noticed it was all farm country in this part of the world. Arriving in Lawrence it was easy to see what Kallie meant. A small town with young people everywhere, mostly students. Arriving at a nice house Kallie said, "This is the rugby house guys." He had arranged for us to stay there and this was great news for us as our funds had dwindled fast in New York.

That afternoon he took us to a local bar called "Johnny's Tavern" which we discovered was the hangout of the rugby club. The owner, a guy called Rick, was involved with of the rugby club so that's why the team hung out here.

Rugby had become pretty popular in America and many clubs drafted foreign players from different countries. The rugby club in Lawrence, Kansas was affiliated with the local university so there were some foreign guys involved. The owner of the rugby pub Johnny's Tavern, set the rugby guys up in big houses they called rugby houses. Here I discovered things were pretty chaotic and it was always party time. In America, especially in a university town keg parties were all the rage. Two or three huge kegs of beer arrived at the house, drinking out of plastic cups everybody got wasted with loud music blaring in the background. Later all you could hear were bedsprings creaking as often the drunken girls spent the night.

The parties at Johnny's Tavern became legendary, especially after the rugby matches. This was a typical American pub with sports memorabilia hanging from the ceiling and walls, a huge bar counter and flashing neon lights with an old time jukebox in the corner. Here we met some of the rugby team and with the old jukebox blaring and a cold beer in our hands, we felt at home amongst these guys. Life here seemed so much more laid back and having a good time was what things were all about.

The next day we went to rugby practice with Kallie, Stefan joined in but I opted to sit on the side line and drink Budweiser instead. The coach turned out to be a South African guy and there were also guys from New Zealand and Australia playing for the team. Rugby was really growing in America and most big cities had rugby teams. I also learnt they had ladies teams too.

A few nights later we dragged a couple of pretty varsity girls home from the bar and I remember Kallie laughing and saying, "This is how we keep fit dudes, by doing human push ups all night long."

For about ten days we hung out with Kallie, really having a great time. Then Stefan suggested that we change our tickets to stay in America a little longer. I had resigned from my job back in South Africa so having no real plans in life, I didn't really need any convincing. Soon after this Stefan bought a small Honda Civic really cheaply from one of the rugby players who was going back home. So now that we had a set of wheels, we decided to drive down to New Orleans and check out this party city that we had heard a lot about.

Arriving in New Orleans we discovered an awesome city with many cool things happening. In the French Quarter we got to discover the local Cajun food. The dishes were spicy and tasted delicious. The local favourite was craw fish which looked like small prawns of sorts and they were cooked in spicy hot sauces. When people talk about being laid back, the people of New Orleans were certainly that and they loved their food and drink. We also discovered the world famous Bourbon Street, the home of the Mardi Gras.

Then one night all of the happy wheels fell off when we found a floating casino and back to my old tricks, I proceeded to get drunk and lose most of the money I had left. The next morning, with a really bad hangover, I realised that I was now up shit creek without a paddle. I had lost my cash and Stefan had no sympathy saying, "You wouldn't listen to me my man so you deal with those burnt fingers."

The trip to New Orleans was an eye opener as South Africa was a rather narrow minded and conservative country in those days. Cheap motels were easy to find and this is where we ended up. We tried to stay as close to the French Quarter as possible. This was all like discovering a new world I thought and a great experience. My biggest regret was having fucked things up in the casino but that's how the cookie crumbled. As I mentioned the people of New Orleans were laid back and chilled out, nothing seemed a problem and having a good time was the thing to be doing.

Finally driving back to Lawrence I realised that my time in America was now over as I had no cash left, the roulette wheel had fucked me over once again.

Six

Back in Lawrence Kallie heard of the loss I had and he said, "Rick from Johnny's knows a guy who owns a lot of these old wooden houses he rents out to the students, he pays guys to paint them so maybe we can get you some work."

The next thing I knew, I was on a ladder two floors up scraping old peeling paint off a house, getting paid ten dollars an hour under the table as legally we couldn't work in America. A week later I had blisters on my hands but dollars back in my pocket and Stefan said, "That should teach you a lesson dude."

Not long after this the snow started to fall, something we were not used to at all coming from South Africa. The snow piled up inches deep and it was crazy. We hadn't seen this before and like little kids we were out there having snowball fights and sledging. This part of the world had lots of snow, the temperature also got incredibly cold and all this snow turned to ice, something else we hadn't experienced before.

One night sitting in Johnny's Tavern one of the rugby guys suggested that we should go and participate in a clinical drug test in Kansas City. Apparently a lot of the rugby guys did this to earn extra cash and for a ten day trial at the clinic they were paid as much as $2000. The guys would check in for ten days and were given some medication, then blood tests were done and evidently it was an easy way to make some cash. Basically they were testing new drugs at this clinic and it was a holiday as you lay in bed and watched TV most of the time.

Discussing this the next day with Stefan he said, "Shit dude two thousand dollars is a fortune."

A week later Stefan and I found ourselves tucked into warm beds in the clinic watching the snow fall outside. It was all really pretty easy but having blood draws eight times a day left my arms covered in huge bruises and this part was no fun. Who knows what drugs we were taking but the cash made it all worthwhile we thought.

Lying in the clinic bed, fate was around the corner and my life was about to change forever.

One afternoon I noticed a guy in the bed across the passage from me watching golf on his TV. Each bed had its own small TV set and this guy was glued to the golf that was on that day. Walking across I introduced myself and meeting Frank Wilson I asked, "Do you play golf?"

Looking at me this guy started laughing and replied, "Shit dude, golf is my life and I'm a professional golf caddie on the PGA Tour in America."

For the next two hours I sat there next to this guy's bed learning all about the world of professional golf.

In America you had the PGA golf tour and only the very best professionals from the world of golf play here for millions of dollars in prize money. Every professional golfer in the world wanted to play on this golf tour and Tiger Woods, having done wonders for the game of golf, also played there. Over in Europe you had the European golf tour and the same applied there. Only the best golfers from the rest of the world played on the European tour. So basically on these two golf tours the top golfers in the world competed for big prize money each week.

Both these tours had many different tournaments each year the only difference was that in Europe these tournaments were held all over the world and in many different countries.

Frank then explained that the PGA Tour in America had a smaller tour for golfers that were trying to progress on to the big PGA Tour. Here you found new guys who had recently turned professional or guys that had fallen off the big tour and they were trying to get back there. This tour also had good prize money and it was really the training ground for up and coming golfers.

Many of the big name pros had graduated from this lower tour, to the big PGA Tour, including guys like the Zach Johnson, Bubba Watson, Nick Watney, Jimmy Walker, Brendan De Jong, and many others. This tour, now called the Web.com Tour, now travelled all across America through many states and at the end of the year the top guys on the money list graduated to the big PGA Tour. This tour was a true test of golf and players had to prove themselves here.

Frank then went on to explain that the same system really applied to all the professional caddies. The top caddies worked for the world's best golfers on either the PGA Tour or the European Tour. These caddies earned huge amounts of money travelling everywhere, living the life of kings. A lot of these caddies were in fact millionaires themselves, getting paid big salaries and good percentages of the prize money. These guys hung on to their "bags" as they call it and they were always in demand when new pro golfers came along.

Caddies hoping to enter this world of professional golf in America normally started to caddie on the Web.com Tour and if they found a good golfer who managed to finish high enough on the money list, the golfer normally kept them on the bag when they went on to play the big PGA Tour.

The player and caddie relationship varied at times as some players had friends on the bag or family members. Others employed good professional tour caddies that had been doing it for years and some chopped and changed caddies, but for the most part, the world's top golfers had the world's top caddies on their bags.

Most of the caddies had nicknames and many people only knew them by these nicknames. Tiger's old caddie was called Fluff, Mickelson's caddie was Bones and so it went. Many of these caddies were good golfers themselves and some had even been professional golfers at some stage in the past.

The bottom line was that these guys actually got paid big money to travel the world walking around the best golf courses, and who could ever think of a better job than that. People worked a whole year to earn a short holiday and these caddies were on a paid holiday all year long. They stayed in great hotels or resorts, ate in expensive restaurants, had fat bank accounts, some had girls in every city, owned fancy houses and cars. What more could a guy wish for?

Sure they knew golf and could guide the professional around a golf course but what a life I thought, sitting there listening to this guy Frank Wilson.

In golf you had the Major tournaments, which carried huge prize money and it was every caddies dream to work at these tournaments, and obviously every golfer's dream to play in the Majors, and only the very best managed to achieve this dream.

Thinking about all this I then asked Frank, "So if there's so much money in this caddie thing what the hell are you doing here acting like a human Guinea pig getting stuck full of holes dude?"

Laughing he then replied, "My mother lives here in Kansas City and she has cancer so I have spent all my money on her medical bills and I'm here for the $2000 so I can get back on the golf tour."

Hearing this I felt bad for having asked this question, as Frank seemed like a nice genuine guy.

That night I lay awake digesting all the things Frank had told me. Waking up the next morning I knew that somehow I was going to become a professional golf caddie.

Up until then I had drifted around aimlessly in life, this sounded like a world I belonged in. I also felt confident that I could master this profession as I had been around golf since a young age.

After breakfast and a few more needle pricks I walked over to Frank and said, "Is there any way you can help me to become a professional golf caddie dude?"

Looking at me he did not say anything for a minute then he replied, "I can't promise you anything but I'm going to Louisiana for the

Louisiana Open on the Web.com Tour and I can try and get you started."

He already knew that I had never been a caddie before but I knew a lot about golf and surely that was good enough for a start in this business.

When I finally discussed this with my buddy Stefan he said, "It sounds too good to be true but you can't work in America legally my man."

I already knew this so I answered, "There are fucking millions of illegal people in America. Do you think one more makes a difference?"

Laughing he replied, "Go for it. What is the worst that can happen, a free ticket home when they catch you?"

* * *

This was always a concern at the back of my mind. One trip with Kenny, a weed-smoking caddie I would shortly meet and travel with, nearly caused me to have a heart attack. Driving from San Diego I noticed that we were approaching a border control and seeing this I started sweating and panicking as I was in the country illegally. I was always aware of the fact that if I was ever caught in America I was going to jail and getting deported. So driving up to a boom at this control point I was holding my breath, my heart was beating a hundred miles per hour. Kenny stopped short of the boom and a guy in a uniform walked out. As I will mention many times throughout my recollections, old Kenny was always smoking weed and stoned. As the guy in uniform approached the car, Kenny's foot slipped off the clutch and the car lunged forward, crashing into the boom.

"What the fuck?" I thought as I saw the border official jump out the way. All hell then broke loose.

They immediately had Kenny out of the car and thank God all the attention was focused on him. After a lot of shouting and chaos, they finally let Kenny go and by that time I was a total nervous wreck. Once again a close call for me but that was always the risk I was running in America.

* * *

Finally leaving the clinic, Stefan was going back to Lawrence and thinking of heading back to South Africa, and I was throwing caution to the wind, staying in America for the time being and joining Frank Wilson on his golf travels.

Seven

Driving down to a town called Lafayette in Louisiana with Frank, home of the Louisiana Open golf tournament, I listened to more golf stories and I felt free as a bird knowing that travelling was the answer in life that I had been searching for. Arriving in Louisiana I got to learn caddie lesson number one. These caddies on this tour knew the cheap hotels closest to the golf course. The money in this business was big but on this tour things were a little different. The caddies all worked on tight budgets sharing a double room to cut the expenses and allow more money for beer. These were all guys trying to get to the big time on the big PGA Tour.

I soon learnt that some of these caddies had been on the PGA Tour before but had lost their jobs, and others were trying to make the jump into the big time for the first time. So Web.com Tour was the stepping-stone to the lucrative world of professional golf both for caddies and players.

Arriving at the cheap hotel we checked in, and following Frank we went to the bar and I got to meet some of the other caddies. These guys were all drinking up a storm and having a good time. I felt right at home amongst these gypsy like characters, that's what they basically were.

At the hotel I met a caddie called Red, who for some reason seemed to like me and said, "I'm sure between us we can get you going dude."

That night a few of the caddies had a poker game going in one of the hotel rooms. It was so much fun, these guys had the weed going and there was booze everywhere. It was honestly just the craziest mix of guys living it up. I just figured out they all loved golf and partying, so this was their life.

By the time I hit the sack that night, I had been accepted into the fold and all these guys assured me that I was going to fit right in. I had never been a weed smoker but that night trying to fit in, I had a few puffs. In the morning I discovered that I had eaten a pizza fit for four people. Frank then informed me that it was called the "Munchies" and he had a good laugh saying, "You are running with the caddies now dude."

Following Frank's advice I got dressed in caddie gear that consisted of a nice golf shirt, shorts and comfortable trainers for all the walking. Frank gave me a great looking cap with "Ping" printed on it and I was all set to become a professional golf caddie, I hoped anyway.

Arriving at the golf course Frank parked in the allocated caddie parking and I followed him as we headed for the clubhouse. Walking past the practice range I saw pros with huge golf bags, all with their names on in bold letters, blasting golf balls in preparation for the week ahead. I must say those golf bags looked huge and mentioning this to Frank he said, "No shit dude, they are heavy."

Arriving at the clubhouse Frank introduced me to a caddie called Kenny who had a long pony tail and a wide floppy hat on his head.

"Welcome brother," Kenny smiled and right from the get go I liked this guy.

All around me I saw caddies walking around with these huge golf bags on their shoulders, and I saw a few golfers that I had actually seen on the TV back in South Africa. This whole scenario was very exciting and standing there I thought, "How the fuck did all this happen?"

Soon afterwards Frank had to leave as he picked up a big Taylor Made golf bag and suddenly I stood there feeling totally lost. All the guys I had met had vanished and all of a sudden I was outside the clubhouse, all by myself not having a clue what to do. All the excitement earlier had suddenly gone and I was out there on my own feeling totally out of place. Trying to look busy I walked around aimlessly starting to think that this had all been a really bad idea. Walking past the putting green I saw Kenny rolling balls back to the golfer and he waved me over.

"Hey dude, go to the players' parking lot and ask any golfer you see if they need a caddie," he said.

I wasn't really sure what he meant but I found the players' parking lot and stood there watching guys arrive unloading big golf bags. The first golfer I approached and asked if he needed a caddie replied, "No thanks, my caddie is here somewhere."

The next guy asked me if I knew the golf course and when I replied that I didn't he said, "Man, you must know the golf course before you look for a job."

Standing there things looked bad and I realized that I was in way above my head. Walking back towards the clubhouse I was totally despondent and uncomfortable, not really knowing what to think or do. I obviously realized that this was not going to be easy and not really knowing these people, or for that matter this business, made things very tough. When I arrived back at the putting green moping along I heard someone shout my name, looking around I saw Red, the guy I had met at the hotel, waving me over.

Walking over to Red he said, "Ok dude, I have got you a golfer to caddie for so you'd better be on your toes."

He then instructed me to go to the practice range and find a golf bag with "Michael Christie" on it. Arriving at the practice range I had butterflies in my stomach as I looked around. I then saw a huge Ping bag with "Michael Christie" in big black letters.

Walking up to the golfer I introduced myself and he said, "Oh you are the guy from South Africa."

We got chatting and he seemed really nice asking me questions and I decided that honesty was the best policy, telling him I wanted to be a caddie but that I had no experience.

"Don't worry," he said, "You know golf so you will pick things up as we go."

Finally I stood there feeling a lot better and it dawned on me that I was now a professional golf caddie. Leaving the practice range I picked up the big Ping bag, it was so heavy and walking along I tried to get it as comfortable as possible on my shoulder. I then learnt that this guy actually played on the big PGA Tour but he had been recovering from an injury. He was playing this tournament as a warm up exercise. This was crazy I remember thinking. Here I had a regular PGA Tour bag on my shoulder and I had never caddied or ever seen this golf course before. I guess in life often things come down to being in the right place at the right time I figured walking along.

That night back at the hotel I was some sort of a celebrity amongst the caddies as they toasted me saying, "You are a professional caddie now," and I made sure I found Red to thank him.

On Tuesday the pros played a practice round and on Wednesday they had a pro-am where they played with the amateur golfers to raise funds for various local charities. During our practice round I learnt a lot but this was golf at another level. These guys hit the ball miles and unbelievably straight. It really was fairways and greens and a pleasure to watch. The heavy bag took some getting used to but I got used to that quickly. The most important job was getting all the yardages correct, learning how far this guy hit every club in his bag.

After the pro-am on Wednesday they had a huge Cajun cook out for everybody at the golf club and thousands of local crawfish were consumed that night. This was a really fun deal as caddies and players mixed with the locals, eating and chatting. When the golf tour hit town it was a big deal and everybody wanted to be part of the action it seemed, especially the local people.

On Thursday, the first day of the tournament, I was very nervous but soon got into the swing of things and my golfer shot a solid 69 playing some really nice golf. Every Friday all golfers had the chance to make the cut and only the top 65 golfers qualified to play Saturday and Sunday for the prize money. So making the weekend was very important in this business. Come Friday my golfer played well once again and we made the cut easily. It was all very exciting to say the least. Watching these professionals it was birdies galore, it was amazing just to be a part of it all, despite the tension and nerves that came with it. However, this was all part of professional golf.

On the Saturday night myself and a few of the caddies went to a local Cajun restaurant for some food and a few beers. I was pleasantly surprised when a pretty waitress told me how much she liked my liked my accent. It doesn't take a genius to work out what happened next. Following her shift at the restaurant she came back to the hotel to pay me a little visit! To me it just summed up my first week on the tour. This was as good as it gets as far as I was concerned.

Come Sunday the leaders were fighting things out in order to try and win the tournament and the big cheque that went with it. My man finally finished inside the top 20 making some decent money for his efforts. Once I had loaded his golf clubs into the back of his car, he handed me a wad of dollars saying, "Thanks for all the help, you will make a good caddie don't worry."

Standing there once he had left, I counted the money and I honestly couldn't believe how much cash I had made for walking around a golf course a few times. I knew then for sure I had found my calling in life and the whole week had been an absolute ball. I just couldn't wait to do it all over again.

*   *   *

The sad part about my first venture into professional golf was hearing that Michael Christie later took his own life. Hearing this was very sad. He was a great guy with a lot of talent. Working for this guy was a pleasure and he had lots to do with me staying in America and becoming a professional caddie. He treated me with respect, making my first steps a lot easier in this tough business. Life has its ups and downs for sure. I still don't know why Michael took his own life, but the golfing world lost a good guy and great player. It was really hard to believe when I heard the bad news later in my travels. I remember this guy being very patient with me as I learnt the ropes of caddying.

Eight

During the week Kenny the ponytail guy had suggested I travel with him to the next tournament in Austin Texas. So leaving Louisiana I had a pocket full of cash and I was off to explore more of America. Driving along Kenny smoked a huge joint and the car was full of a heavy smoke. After my pizza ordeal I was not getting involved with this stuff again.   During my time with Kenny, I noticed the more stoned this guy got the more he talked. He was so funny to listen to but I had no chance of sleeping. Not long into the journey my ears were ringing but hey it was his car after all. I also figured out that Kenny was an old school hippie type, he had been smoking weed nearly all his life.

Arriving in Austin it was the same caddie drill, finding a cheap hotel near the golf course. It was here I discovered a fun city with lots of great bars and clubs everywhere. The bars usually had live music as lots of local bands played in them on a regular basis. The girls had great accents and they looked so hot in their cowboy boots and tight jeans. Here you could eat the best steaks and all the various barbecue food you could imagine. For me, Texas had a very old fashioned charm about it. The people were loud but very nice and everybody seemed to have loads of money in this neck of the woods.

Arriving at the golf course I was back in the parking lot looking for a bag. I was a lot more confident about getting one this time. About two hours later, a professional called Bryan Gorman hired me and knowing how things worked it was all a lot easier this time.

Rooming with Kenny was a new experience as he insisted on smoking his weed in the room and he drove me nuts with all his chatting. Apart from that he was ok to deal with but as he didn't drink any alcohol, we didn't actually hang out together that much.

On the golf course I had the caddie thing under control and come Friday amazingly my golfer had his name on the leaderboard.

Saturday morning the heavens opened up flooding the golf course and play was suspended for the day. Come Sunday it was the same story and finally the tournaments was reduced to 36 holes. This all resulted in my golfer finishing on the leaderboard and here I made a nice amount of cash. I honestly wondered what could be easier than this caddying job. However, I now knew the secret to this business was to find a good golfer and hold on to the bag for as long as possible. Being the new guy on the block this would take some time but I had my ears and eyes open at all times.

I then learnt that the next tournament was supposed to be back in Louisiana, the "Shreveport Open". However, due to serious amounts of rain, it had been postponed. I hadn't really planned for a tournament being postponed and now it seemed I was stuck in Texas. Kenny then decided to visit some friends that lived on a farm not too far away and he invited me along. I knew that this had to be some sort of hippie type deal with lots weed smoking, but having nowhere else to go I accepted his offer but wasn't really looking forward to it. Driving along we eventually came to a small town called Lake Charles and I noticed a big neon sign-saying hotel and casino.

I then asked Kenny if we could stop here for a break and not really keen he said, "Ok but only for an hour, then we hit the road."

Walking into the casino I cashed in a few hundred dollars and ordered a double Captain Morgan from the pretty waitress who remarked on my cool accent. I gave Kenny some cash to go get himself some food and I hit the roulette table. For a change, from the very start I hit some of my regular numbers and I soon had a healthy pile of chips on the table. By the time I ordered the next cocktail I had chatted to the pretty waitress a bit and I knew if I had more time I could have a real good look at the big boobs she was revealing through a half unbuttoned blouse.

When Kenny made an appearance after his dinner, I had won maybe a thousand dollars. The cocktails had me buzzing and the last thing I wanted to do was to leave.

"Hey Kenny, how about we stay here tonight and I will pay for a nice room," I said.

Looking at all my chips he replied, "No way dude, cash in and let's get going."

I asked him again to hang out longer and next thing we got into an argument.

"You fucking stay here but I'm leaving," he finally said storming off.

I honestly thought that he would cool down and come back, so I kept on gambling and drinking. This was always the problem with addicted gamblers as they never knew when to leave a casino and I had been dealing with this problem for a long time. Always ending up in the shit and this time was not going to be any different.

After this I didn't remember too much about what happened after my argument with Kenny, but when I woke up in a hotel bed with a naked girl I knew I was in trouble. With my head throbbing I jumped into my clothes and rushed downstairs into the parking lot. I frantically ran around looking for Kenny's car but soon realized he had left without me. Sitting down on the sidewalk I had my head between my hands realizing that I was stuck there with no clothes or anything. For that matter, I also knew that every time I set foot in a fucking casino the shit always hit the fan.

In a panic I then stood up and digging around in my pockets, thank God I discovered a thick wad of dollars. So at least I had not lost all my cash this time. From here I headed back into the hotel lobby and I ordered two cups of strong black coffee. Sipping the coffee I knew the only option I really had was to hop on a bus and go back to Lawrence and hope Stefan or Kallie were still around. I then decided to make the best of a bad situation; I went back upstairs and got rid of my frustration on the naked waitress.

That afternoon with a hangover from hell I found myself sitting amongst a bunch of dirty, loud Mexicans on a Greyhound bus thinking about how badly I had fucked things up. By the time I arrived in Lawrence I looked and smelt like a bum. Catching a taxi I headed for the rugby house. Arriving there I saw the Honda parked outside and knocking, Stefan opened the front door.

"What the hell happened to you?" he shouted, as if I was a ghost standing there.

Once inside I told him the whole crazy story and by then he was laughing his head off saying, "What is it with you and those fucking useless casinos man."

Once I had cleaned up we went shopping for new clothes and Stefan informed me that he was going back to South Africa. He asked what my plans were and I told him that I was going back to the golf tour.

I spent some time hanging out with the guys but soon after I had a schedule planned for the remainder of the year. I said goodbye to Stefan and jumped back on a Greyhound bus, this time on my way to Richmond, Virginia to join the golf tour again. When I eventually arrived at the golf course, all the caddies knew the story from a few weeks earlier, as Kenny had told them all about the "crazy South African".

When I bumped into Kenny later he was still mad at me saying, "You are one crazy fucking dude."

I was happy to get my stuff back and at the same time, relieved as my passport was also in my bag.

Nine

It was during the week in Richmond Virginia with Kenny the Weed Smoker that he had a bag full of golf balls on the carpet of our hotel room. He was trying chip them onto the bed and into the bin with a wedge. I said to him that he had to stop as he was going to break something. Stoned as usual he laughed and said "Relax I know what I'm doing." The next thing I knew, he caught a ball thin, blading it straight through the big glass window and out into the parking lot. I started shouting at him, I told him he shouldn't be doing it and now we were going to be in deep shit. The next thing I see is him running outside and I wondered to myself what the hell he was doing. From outside he started throwing all the glass pieces back into the room and I remember thinking that he'd lost his mind. Once all the glass was back on the hotel room floor, he called the front desk and shouting at the top of his voice asked to speak to the manager.

I honestly thought Kenny had gone mad and when the manager came to the phone Kenny shouted, "What kind of establishment is this? Someone just threw a stone through my hotel room window," and then I noticed he had a big rock in his hand.

The manager rushed up to the room and apologised profusely, moving us to a much bigger deluxe room and said, "I'm so sorry guys, this room is complimentary," I started laughing to myself as Kenny had come up with the best plan in the world.

Afterwards Kenny said, "That's called thinking on your feet" and I had to reply "No Shit."

*   *   *

In Richmond I hooked up with a caddie called Texas Dan and for the next few weeks we travelled together.

That week I got very lucky according to everybody as I got hired by a hot shot golfer called Matt Gogel, whom many tipped to be on the PGA Tour the following year. He was high on the money list and it was a prize bag I was told. The only problem here was that the guy told me that he had no sponsor so he couldn't pay me any percentage money. However, he said that if I accepted this deal he would keep me on his bag the following year if he graduated to the big PGA Tour. So it really was a gamble and deciding to look at the big picture I took the job.

That very first week ended up costing me a lot of cash, as come Sunday Gogel finished in fifth place and all I earned was my weekly salary.

I remember Kenny saying to me afterwards, "You really are a crazy South African. How can you work for no percentage money? That's what all the caddies work for and look how much cash you just threw away dude."

I guess he was right but a chance to work on the PGA Tour was hard to turn down. The up side was that Gogel was moving higher up the money list so I stuck to my guns and stayed on the bag.

For a few tournaments things went well enough and I was having fun travelling all over America experiencing many different things in different towns and cities. I had learnt a lot about professional golf by then and most weeks I found time to play some golf myself. Many of the caddies were keen and good golfers and they played a lot in their spare time. Off the course I hung out with the caddies going to bars and restaurants at night. I was really living the American dream, I was doing it all, though I was doing it all as a migrant South African caddie, but who gave a shit.

On the golf tour I always felt safe as guys from all over the world played on the tour. So coming from another country was not out of the ordinary. I also discovered that some of these caddies were real characters and some weeks all sorts of crazy shit happened. Guys ended up in jail for getting drunk and disorderly, some got into shit for phoning the escort service from the hotel and then not paying the girls, others got thrown out of nightclubs for being drunk. It was really a travelling circus at times.

*   *   *

At the tournament in Virginia Beach, I can recall two caddies that rented bicycles in order to get around the town. They would ride these bikes from bar to bar to avoid getting a D.U.I. One evening, after getting so drunk, they forgot where they had parked these bicycles, never finding them. The company that rented these to them demanded that they were paid for. This definitely left a dent in their pockets that week

It was also at in Virginia Beach where some serious drama unfolded. I was sharing a room with a caddie called Freddy and we were staying on the beachfront. One afternoon the wind was howling coming from the sea. Sitting on our balcony with the sliding door open the wind was blowing into the room fiercely. Freddy had been smoking a joint on the balcony and he told me he was going downstairs to the shop attached to the hotel. The next thing I heard was the front door slam shut with a loud bang, and then I heard Freddy scream. Jumping up I ran into the room and saw Freddy standing there, holding his one hand with blood everywhere.

"Pick up my finger," he shouted at me and looking down I saw the tip of his one finger lying on the floor.

The wind had slammed the front door shut catching his finger and slicing the tip off. I picked up the piece of finger in a towel and rushing downstairs I found some ice to wrap it up in. The ambulance arrived soon afterwards and Freddy was rushed to hospital where they tried to sew the finger back on again. This was a crazy and scary experience. I told Freddy afterwards it was a good thing that he was stoned at the time, as I am sure he did not fully realise what had happened. Needless to say he became known as "Freddy The Finger" on the golf tour. This guy actually had been Zack Johnson's first caddie and I remember back then Freddy telling me that this guy was the real deal.

*   *   *

When the tour arrived in Greenville South Carolina, the first of my problems on the tour surfaced as a crazy thing happened that week. By now I had witnessed and experienced the highs and lows of professional golf. I had seen players go nuts, throwing and slamming clubs, swearing and shouting when things went wrong. Some of these guys took their anger and frustrations out on their caddies but what happened that week was totally out of order I thought.

On Thursday, playing great golf, my player shot a low score to lead the tournament. Friday, he kept it going to stay on the leaderboard and things were looking good leading in to the weekend. In good spirits I joined the boys in a local bar that night playing pool and having a good time. Then Saturday came, suddenly out of nowhere, the wheels seemed to fall off as my player started hitting the ball all over the map, playing really bad golf. I could see that he was at boiling point and finally shooting 77 he stormed off the golf course, mad as hell.

On Sunday it was the same story with everything going wrong and finally with a few holes left to play I said, "Don't worry man, we will get them next week." I knew that this guy had been having a nightmare out there, so I figured a little encouragement would help.

Suddenly this guy exploded like a bomb, walking up to me shouting, "Shut the hell up, your job is to carry that bag, do you get me?"

As I've said, I had seen golfers abuse they caddies before but I sure as hell wasn't going to let that happen to me. So I shouted back, "Well your job is to go find another fucking caddie," and I marched off without saying another word on the golf course. Walking off the 18th green I threw his golf bag on the ground and simply walked away.

So that was the end of my days on this golf bag. Hearing the story most of the caddies said, "Good for you. Who do some of these pros fucking think they are anyway?"

I guess out on the tour most of the guys were great. However, some of the pros could be real arseholes too. All caddies understand this fine line between a pay cheque and unemployment and some would maintain silence in order to keep on the favourable side of that line.

* * *

I recall an incident on the PGA Tour where on one hole all of the golfers hit their tee shots into the fairway and were playing into the green with their second. On this golf course the rough around the greens was really bad and really thick, so missing a green meant the ball sank to the bottom of the rough and it left a tricky chip shot. Once the golfers had played their second shots we all marched up to the green and as was normal practice, we all lay the big golf bags down on the grass beside the green.

Arriving on the green one of the golfers couldn't find his ball and he went mad saying, "That shot was straight at the flag".

We all searched in the thick rough around the green looking everywhere but amazingly nobody could find this player's ball. When the five minutes were up the golfer, angry and muttering to himself declared the ball lost and headed back down the fairway. Finally, after watching him make a double bogey on the hole we picked up the golf bags and moved towards to the next hole. When the caddie next to me picked up his players bag, low and behold lying under the bag was the player's ball we'd been looking for. This caddie had put the bag down right on top of the player's golf ball behind the green.

Seeing the ball I said to the other caddie, "Shit what now?" and shrugging his shoulders he bent down and picked up the ball. He then looked away and just stuck it in his pocket. I wasn't sure what to say or do. Then, walking to the next tee box the other caddie threw this ball into the trash can, I couldn't believe what I saw.

Arriving at the tee box he then said to me, "You did not see anything OK."

I wasn't sure what the hell to say anyway but I sure as hell hadn't done anything wrong. As things turned out, come Sunday this caddie's golfer finished only two shots behind the winner, and laying down the golf bag on his player's ball had in fact cost him a chance of winning.

Ten

After the whole recent drama of walking away from my player, I bounced around on different bags without much success on the golf course, but I was travelling and exploring America so that was good enough for me. By the time the golf season ended I had been across most of America and had experienced many cool things, so in many ways I felt blessed and lucky. I had also decided that I was going to stay in America and caddie again the following year. I knew that I had learnt enough to be a good tour caddie and the dream of getting to the big time and the big money was alive for sure.

I now saw caddies I had lived and travelled with on their way to the big PGA Tour and I knew I was a good enough caddie to follow them. The only missing piece of the puzzle was finding the golfer who was good enough to make the jump on to the big PGA Tour and take me with him.

So during the off season I headed back to Lawrence and the snow that came with it, but by then both Kallie and Stefan were long gone. Arriving back in Lawrence, Kansas, the whole scene had changed as most of the guys I knew had left and whilst in a bar, I bumped into a guy called Jerry that I had met before. He invited me to stay at his house for a few weeks. This guy Jerry was a very outspoken and loud character and he knew a lot of people around town. The times I got to hang out with him he flashed the dollars and he certainly liked the high life. I remember just outside Lawrence a guy and his wife owned a large farm and you could see they had big money. I knew that this Jerry was a high roller and on a few occasions I went with him to hang out on the farm with his friends. I became suspicious that Jerry was supplying them with cocaine, and I was soon to discover that he was, in fact, a big time drug dealer.

In America I had discovered that weed was widely used but I also realized people used a lot of other drugs too. I honestly thought that Jerry was just a regular guy choosing to make a living this way. I later discovered that he was hooked himself and this changed my whole outlook on things. So there I was, living with a drug dealer but he was actually a really cool guy and as I saw it, his business was his business and I would just stay out of it. Jerry had a lady friend called Donna who I got involved with for a while and the days mostly consisted of hanging out and relaxing as Jerry took care of us. However, the night I came home and found Jerry passed out in a chair with a needle in his arm I knew it was time to fuck off. I was having no part of that shit and I spent my last days hanging out at Donna's place before moving on and finding a new place to stay.

*　*　*

During my time in Lawrence I had also met a guy called Dan who had flunked out of the university and we became really good friends. Once he had heard all about my caddie travels, he was really keen to do the same. He asked me if I could take him out on the golf tour. I figured that Frank Wilson had helped me so why couldn't I help this guy.

Eleven

When the new golf season arrived I found myself sitting next to Dan on the Greyhound bus on our way back to Louisiana. Arriving back on the golf tour I introduced Dan to everyone and he seemed to fit in great. It was then time to get busy looking for a good golfer to caddie for that season.

I knew a South African player called Deanne Pappas from the previous year so I approached him at the entrance to the golf club and he hired me. This soon turned out to be a great move as finally I got into the mix, having a chance of winning my first golf tournament. Starting out I had a few good results on this bag and a few weeks later, at the Shreveport Open in Louisiana come Sunday, we were leading the tournament. I now had a real shot at being on a winning bag. Sunday, with large crowds following us, I had butterflies in my stomach. This was what it was all about; having a chance of winning tournaments, and finally being there was a great feeling.

After the first nine holes Pappas clung to the lead and it was some tense and dramatic stuff. Coming down the stretch he slipped a little and finally standing on the 18th tee box he needed a birdie to get into a play off and give himself a chance to win, along with two other guys that were already in the clubhouse. This hole was a reachable par 5 so I fancied our chances as this guy smashed the ball miles.

After a really good drive, I got to the ball as quickly as possible in order to get his yardage. Once I had it worked out, all he had left was a 4 iron into the green so I thought it was looking good. The only problem was around this green you had a run off area into a deep gully of sorts. So basically, if he did not hold the green with the second shot, the up and down was going to be a tricky one for a birdie.

When Pappas finally hit the second shot it looked perfect in the air, it was straight at the flag the whole time. However, it took an awful bounce once it landed, sending it into the gully over the back of the green and into a very awkward position. Approaching the 18th green the large crowd was cheering and clapping and it was all some really exciting stuff. The whole time I was praying that this guy could perform some sort of miracle shot and get the ball to finish somewhere near the flag, but I knew it was going to be close to impossible.

Deciding on a flop shot, the best Pappas could do was getting the ball to rest roughly 10 feet from the flag. Standing over this putt the crowd had gone silent; my heart was beating like never before. I was so nervous I could barely watch. Holding the flagstick I watched the ball for what felt like an age as it rolled towards the hole. As it got closer I honestly thought he had made it but it caught the edge of the hole and sadly lipped out, ending any chance that we had of winning that week. We ended up finishing third and this was still a great result. Above all else, what an experience to be a part of.

That night Pappas joined us as we visited one of the big casinos in town. We got so drunk that I eventually slept on his hotel room floor, not being able to get back to my hotel. By now, my buddy Dan had provided some entertainment for everyone involved on the tour. During the tournament he had pulled a compass from his pocket to read the direction of the wind. Being new to the tour he wasn't aware but this was strictly prohibited and as a result, he got his golfer disqualified from the tournament. To make things worse, his player at the time was on the leaderboard. From that day on, Dan was called "Due North" on the tour, and that name has stuck with him ever since.

*   *   *

While mentioning Dan's nickname I am reminded of Rob Johnson, brother of PGA professional Richard, and how he earned his Tour nickname. Rob caddied on the tour on and off for a few years, but I always felt the real reason for this was that it afforded an opportunity to follow and watch his brother. Rob was almost ten years younger than Richard and always looked up to him, they had a close relationship and Rob was by far his biggest fan. On the few occasions we roomed together during tournaments, Rob would always be on the laptop checking his brother's stats and scorecards. It was while I was rooming with Rob that he was given his nickname on the tour. During the Mark Christopher Charity Classic in 2006 Rob had flown in to Los Angeles to watch his brother. Once he arrived he decided to try and get a bag with one of the players and make a little money while he was there. Monday morning we headed to golf course, which was called Empire Lakes in Rancho Cucamonga, California. I headed to the range and started work before going to walk the course, whilst Rob stood in the car park hoping to pick somebody up. Sure enough, within the hour, I spotted Rob heading to the range with a bag on his back. He'd got a job working for David Sutherland for the week.

We decided to share a room as it would keep the costs down and it was a great laugh all week. On the Tuesday, we decided to walk the course together and check all the yardages, which, was always easier when two or three of you were doing it. Wednesday for the most part was spent on the driving range or the short game area, as generally this was the day the Pro Am was played. It was no different for us this week, we watched our players hit balls and do some fine tuning before heading back to the hotel for some carpet golf. This was played by a lot of the caddies when they had nothing else to do. We used to putt balls from one end of the room to the other into small drinking glasses for money. Being the gambler I was, I always used to take Rob on, with usually very little success.

Thursday morning we headed to the course to start the tournament, both hoping for a good week so we could get a big cheque and have some fun. Rob was so excited before he started. He loved golf more than anything and couldn't wait to get going. Richard started with a 71, which wasn't the best, but he still had a chance of making the cut. Sutherland started with a 65 and Rob was so thrilled to be towards the top of the leaderboard. The next day something happened which I will never forget and subsequently landed Rob with his nickname. After a steady front nine holes on Friday, Sutherland played his approach shot to the 10th green. Both his playing partners missed the green therefore Rob thought it would be the perfect time to stop and use the portable bathroom that the spectators used. By the time he had finished, the group were down on the green. He started jogging towards the green when a tournament volunteer approached on a cart and offered him a lift to avoid Sutherland waiting for him. On the back nine, they kept playing steady golf and by the end of their round they were still in the top ten after shooting a 71 ... then the shit hit the fan.

David Sutherland was then approached by a rules official asking if his caddie had taken a ride on a cart. Sutherland responded with no, as he wasn't aware of what Rob did and had his back turned towards him while he was on it. The rules official then continued to say that people had reported seeing his caddie on a cart. Just as the cards were about to be signed Sutherland called Rob over and said that people have accused him of taking a ride on a cart. It must have been one of the hardest things Rob has done but he had to confess. He had no idea this was against the rules. It cost Sutherland a two-stroke penalty and knocked him way back down the leaderboard. Rob told me the story back at the room and described how Sutherland got really angry.

He said to Rob, "You can work the weekend, but you won't work for me again".

Rob was devastated as he cost his player a lot of money, Richard missed the cut after shooting 73 in the second round, and all of a sudden, this week was not looking like being so much fun. I'll always remember this story, and this is the reason the caddies named Rob "The Hitch Hiker".

As it went, we continued to travel across America and my man Pappas kept moving up the money list. He looked good to make the move on to the big PGA Tour the next year. Finally I had a great steady bag, with a good guy and things were looking great for me. I had all sorts of cash and off the course Dan, or rather Due North, and I had great times hanging out and chasing the ladies.

*   *   *

While traveling in America working on the golf tours the caddies always tried to play golf when they found a gap. Most golf clubs would let the caddies play for free or maybe just charged a cart fee. One week Due North and I were visiting his brother in St Louis and we decided to go and play some golf. Dan called a golf club and speaking to the club pro he said we travelled on the PGA Tour. They were very happy to accommodate us, I borrowed some golf clubs and off we went.

Arriving at the golf course the club pro said it was an honour to have two PGA Tour players at his golf course. Hearing this I nearly burst out laughing as we were just caddies, normally if we broke 80 we were doing well. The club pro then said that he had arranged for the club champion to play with us. Dan then made things worse by going along with this and telling him that I was a professional golfer that had travelled all the way from South Africa.

I whispered to Dan "Are you fucking crazy or what?"

By now I could not change this whole bullshit story and I was in a flat panic standing on the first tee and about to play with the club champion. The really crazy thing was that I somehow managed to shoot an even par front nine, which was a miracle. At the halfway house Dan told me the club champion had said that I had some game and I started laughing, as I was maybe a nine handicap at best.

On the back nine my true colours came out as the wheels fell off and I shot a 42 feeling a total fool and looking like one at the same time. I wondered what the club champion had to be thinking and we couldn't leave the golf club fast enough after the round. This was all really crazy but we did eventually have a good laugh about it.

*   *   *

When the tour arrived in Knoxville Tennessee the golfing gods were to change their minds. Here we discovered busy country and western dance clubs. They were filled with super-hot girls in tight jeans and boots doing a dance they called "line-dancing". Everybody made the same moves to country music and it was amazing that all these people knew the exact same steps. Guys and girls crowded and dance floors doing this dance.

One night after some cocktails I tried to give it a go but some girl said to me, "Sorry dude, but you don't have a clue," and that was the end of my line-dancing career.

Once the tournament got started my man Pappas fired on all cylinders once again, shooting up the leaderboard and come Friday I got to witness golf of the very highest quality. This guy made birdies galore that day, and finally playing the last hole he needed a birdie to shoot 62 and to set a new course record. By now he was on top of the leaderboard and totally in the zone as they call it.

The green on this hole was elevated so you couldn't see it from the fairway and Pappas hit a great tee shot, the ball was in perfect shape down the middle.

Once we worked out the yardage for the second shot Pappas said, "It's a solid 7 iron."

Looking around at the clouds and trees, I noticed that the wind had picked up blowing into us, so I said, "No it's the 6 iron, the wind is stronger now."

Suddenly Pappas seemed puzzled and he said, "Are you sure?"

I finally talked him into hitting the 6 iron and arriving on the green my heart sank into my shoes.

"What were you thinking?" Pappas shouted, "I told you it was a 7 iron".

The ball had pitched pin high and bounced off the green into some thick rough. This guy was mad, kicking his golf bag and I knew I had big shit on my hands. The chip was impossible and finally making a bogey Pappas stormed off into the clubhouse. The fact that he had just posted an awesome 64 seemed to be lost now and I had a bad feeling more shit was to follow.

The next morning the local newspaper carried a headline saying, "Caddie cost Pappas new course record."

Reading this, I knew then that this guy was going to fire me and come Sunday he had dropped off the leaderboard. Once we had finished he said how he couldn't afford to make mistakes like this, so I was back in the parking lot looking for a new bag. In this business it was often such a fine line between the right and wrong club and obviously getting it wrong lost me a good job.

Twelve

The week after parting company with Pappas the tour had a week off, so wanting to forget all about golf for now, Due North and myself joined a few other caddies and went to hang out up in the Smoky Mountains, in a town called Gatlinburg. Arriving there we discovered an amazing little town nestled high up in the beautiful mountain country. All week we played golf, went shopping at the huge outlet malls nearby and hung out in the local bars. The Friday night there was a party at one of the bars and sitting at the bar I noticed a very pretty blonde woman sitting with a much older guy.

Somehow we got chatting and I discovered they were from Florida and were taking a holiday. They were married but she was obviously a lot younger than her husband. When the music started, to my surprise she grabbed my hand and pulled me onto the dance floor. Soon she was rubbing her boobs up against me, and feeling totally awkward I kept looking at the husband wondering what the hell he had to be thinking.

Finally sitting down again, the woman went to the ladies' room and leaning towards me the husband said, "No worries man, you can screw my wife if you want to. She seems to like you."

Hearing this I nearly choked on my beer but he carried on saying, "We have a very open marriage and we like to play on the side."

One crazy situation to be caught up in I thought, but after a lot more beers I started to like this arrangement they had. It all finally turned out that we went back to their hotel room in the early hours and banging the wife, the husband sat in a chair watching.

Telling the story the next day, Due North laughed saying, "You're lucky you don't have a sore arse dude," and maybe he was right I thought.

*　　*　　*

After a fun week we all headed back to the golf tour and I was looking for a job again. As bad as things turned out, some good luck came along as another South African golfer called Marco Gortana hired me. Then my luck got even better as arriving in Salt Lake City, Utah for a tournament, I had another shot at being on a winning bag. Here this guy played some great golf and come Sunday we had a large crowd and TV cameras following us. We were playing in the last group and lying in second place.

I had been in this position before so I knew what to expect and it was the same tense dramatic stuff trying to win. The leader Carl Paulson was on fire that day but Gortana kept him in within his sights. Finally walking on to the 18th green the usual cheering from the grandstand greeted us. The best my man could do here was make a par and finish second. This resulted in a nice bonus and I was back in the pound seats. This was however the last tournament Gortana played any good and soon after the golf season came to an end.

Due North had not had much luck on the tour but according to him he had learnt a lot anyway. So once more we headed back to the snow and cold in Lawrence, Kansas. This time we found a student's house to stay in and Due North found a job making pizzas for the off-season. I got to eat all the free pizza I wanted. Once it was finally time to leave Lawrence, I honestly never wanted to see a pizza again.

I knew things were blowing hot and cold for me on the golf tour but I just couldn't find the right guy to make the move on to the big PGA Tour for some reason. I went back out on the golf tour for the next few seasons but it was always the same old story with moments of glory but never finding a player that made the jump to the big tour. Due North experienced the same thing and by then I had seen most of America. My family back home thought I had gone mad not returning to South Africa.

Many of my caddie buddies were now on the big PGA Tour earning big cash but I just couldn't find a way there.

Thirteen

Going back on the tour once again things finally changed as I started to work for a guy called Richard Johnson. This guy came from Wales and had married an American girl. You couldn't find a nicer guy to caddie for. We clicked right from the get go and we were to have some great moments together. Apart from working together I hung out with him and his family a lot. He had two awesome brothers that often came to America to visit him. I guess you could say I became part of the family and we had many great times travelling across America together. The first year I worked for this guy we had some chances to win with a few top ten finishes in tournaments.

*　　*　　*

Playing the BMW tournament in Greenville, South Carolina one week, Richard Johnson's brother Geoff had come over from Wales to visit and watch the golf. Richard had organized a big house up on the mountain for the family and myself to stay in that week. Old Freddy The Finger also stayed with us as Richard always had time for the caddies. One night we all went out for dinner and a few drinks and Geoff and Freddy got wasted. After a good night we left with Geoff and Freddy telling us they were going to stay a while and come back later. Arriving at the house we waited a few hours but there was no sign of them returning. We then started to get really worried about them, but all of a sudden we heard them enter the house. When they finally came into the room we were all sitting in, they were both white as ghosts and shaken up. We then learned that Freddy had stupidly driven back. Not only that, he had driven into the back of another car and of all things it was a fucking police car. Telling the story, a drunk Geoff started laughing so hard he ended up rolling on the floor. Soon we were all laughing apart from Freddy. The only reason he didn't end up in jail was because the police officer was a keen golfer, and Freddy promised to get him tickets to the tournament. The next day Geoff told us it was the scariest, yet funniest thing he'd ever seen in his life.

*   *   *

That year the tour had a new tournament called the Monterey Open near Pebble Beach. Clint Eastwood himself lived nearby and he was heavily involved with the tournament. Arriving in Monterey we went to visit Pebble Beach and what an awesome place this was, located along a very scenic coastline. As far as golf courses went, this place had to be one of the most scenic and best golf courses in the world I thought.

The winner of the Monterey Open was to be given a spot to play in the AT&T National Pro-Am at Pebble Beach on the big PGA tour the following year. This was a huge incentive for players and the Monterey Open was played on a golf course called "The Bayonet Course". This was one of the toughest golf courses in America so the Monterey Open was going to be survival of the fittest it seemed.

During the pro-am only three players had managed to break par and everybody was talking about how tough this golf course was.

The first two rounds Richard played steady golf to make the cut but he was a couple over par and in the middle of the field. On Saturday he played good golf to get things back to one over par but a golfer called Pat Perez had somehow surged ahead at six under par. This was amazing as only three players were under par going into the final round on Sunday. Arriving at the golf course we found ourselves seven shots behind the leader and a top 10 finish was wishful thinking at best.

Sunday, Richard found game I'd never seen before, playing unbelievable golf and starting way behind the leaders he shot a great

53

68 to get it to three under par for the tournament. Hopefully a top 10 finish we were thinking. Sitting in the clubhouse we learnt that Pat Perez was having a nightmare out on the golf course and all the leaders were struggling. Suddenly out of nowhere Richard's name had shot up the leaderboard and we couldn't believe our eyes.

"That's nuts. Can you believe those guys are falling apart," Richard said to me watching the leaderboard.

Finally only one golfer coming in could still win the tournament and everybody was speechless as the leaders had all fallen away and Richard Johnson stood on top of the leaderboard. When the only person that could beat Richard missed a short putt on the 18th hole, amazingly from nowhere Richard had won the Monterey Open. It was all so crazy. We were both in a state of shock to say the least.

When Clint Eastwood himself presented Richard with the trophy, I started to realise that we had just won the fucking Monterey Open and this meant I was going to caddie on the big PGA Tour at Pebble Beach. I also realized that I had made a lot of cash and I wondered what my old buddy Stefan would say if he knew what had just happened.

Afterwards, Richard still trying to digest it all said, "Can you believe this shit mate?" and laughing I replied, "Well we get to visit Pebble Beach again and play against Mr Woods. How fucking cool is that mate?"

We also then realized that he had shot up the money list and a full time spot on the big PGA Tour was now on the cards.

Once the prize giving was complete and Richard had finished doing all the interviews that he was obligated to do, it was time for a couple of beers and a celebration. Shit I had won on tour for the first time and had made a lot of cash. Richard's younger brother Rob was also caddying at this tournament, he was working for Vaughn Taylor and they unfortunately missed the cut after rounds of 73, 73. As Richard was so far back going into the final round, Rob decided to make the fifteen-hour drive to the next tournament in Albuquerque, New Mexico. This way he could get a hotel room booked for us next to the golf course. As soon as Richard was able to he called Rob to give him the news; I could hear Rob's scream of celebration from the passenger seat I was sitting in. As his biggest fan, Rob couldn't believe what had happened.

Once Richard had finished talking to Rob he handed me the phone, "We've done it brotha," I shouted.

I told Rob not to book a room once he got to Albuquerque as the room that week was on me. I said I would call him with the hotel details to check in the following morning. It was an unwritten rule with the caddies that if you win on the tour you pay for your roommate's hotel the next week. Rob had always helped me if I was short of cash when we were travelling so I was looking forward to getting us nice digs for the week, and giving him a little something back. After a few beers that night celebrating with Richard, I met up with a couple of the other caddies for a drink. One drink led to another, another let to another, and those led me to the casino. Thankfully I didn't have my entire winning bonus in my pocket, as there is no doubt I would have lost that too. I did however part with a large amount of cash and woke up in the morning with a pounding head. I reached to the bedside table to grab my cell phone and saw that I had lots of missed calls from Rob.

"Shit!" I yelled out loud, Rob was calling to find out which hotel I booked.

I obviously hadn't booked anything, so I quickly got onto the computer in the hotel lobby and looked for places. Richard told me he was staying in the Candlewood Suites that week. The Candlewood Suites were lovely, fairly expensive but a lot nicer than what we usually stayed in. However, the fact I was so hung over and feeling sorry for myself after losing a load of cash, I went for a cheaper motel just down the road. I quickly called Rob and gave him the address and check in details, so he could go to the room when he finished at the course.

A few hours later as I started making my way to Albuquerque, I had a text message from Rob saying, "What the fuck is this motel Pierre?"

Head in my hands, I knew I had messed up. This motel was going to be awful I could sense it. It was about midnight when I finally arrived in Albuquerque, still hung over but on a massive high after the previous day's overwhelming experience. I was upset with myself that I had lost to the casino again, however this was beginning to feel like an everyday occurrence. Thankfully Richard knew what I was like and refused to give me my big bonus in one hit. Some would argue that this was unfair but Richard did this for my benefit. As much as I needed the cash, I always knew how honest and what a great guy Richard was and knew I would get it when I needed it. After all he had just won nearly $100,000. I was sure he was good for it. As I walked towards the motel door I could hear all sorts of commotion from outside. I knocked once but there was no answer, I knocked again a little louder and Rob opened the door.

"What the hell have you booked us in to?" he shouted.

Dan one of the other caddies was in the room with Rob as they were trying to play a little carpet golf for some cash. The problem was the room was infested with cockroaches. They were all over the place.

Rob looked at me and said, "There is no way I'm staying here brotha".

He was right though. I may well have booked us into the worst motel in Albuquerque if not fucking America. All because of that magnetic force that the casino had on me. We tried another room but it was just as bad so Rob said he was leaving and decided to get a room in the Candlewood Suites for the evening, the same hotel that his brother was staying in. He was angry, as by this time it was almost 2am and he had to be at the course by 7am. I couldn't believe how I had let him down. Rob had done lots for me when my pockets were empty. I was sorry beyond belief but it was just another tale of how gambling let another person down in my life. Luckily the next evening we did find a half decent hotel to stay in. It even had nice level carpet so the putting in the room continued. You can guess the outcome.

Fourteen

By the time the year-ending Tour Championship arrived we knew a good finish here would secure Richard the PGA Tour card for the following year.

The Pebble Beach tournament was played early the next year so we had a lot going on. Only the top guys on the money list got to play in the Tour Championship so these guys were all fighting it out at this last tournament to get onto the big PGA Tour.

I travelled to Dothan Alabama with a caddie buddy "Mountain" Mike. Mountain was a full-bearded hulk of a guy who looked like he was straight from the back woods, and who had been known to loop a complete 18 with two fully loaded tour bags without ever breaking stride or sweat.

Arriving in Dothan, Mountain and I searched for a hotel near the golf course and walking into the City Lodge a pretty blue-eyed girl greeted us from behind the reception counter. She seemed to be very friendly and chatty, helping us book into the hotel and asking me a few questions about South Africa after seeing my passport. Getting to our room Mountain said, "Trust me my man, we are both going to bonk that girl," and I thought he was dreaming.

A little later Mountain went back to the reception and about an hour later he returned with a huge grin.

"What did I tell you?" he said. "She is coming here for cocktails when she knocks off dude."

We then went shopping, buying snacks and booze to have in the room, and unbelievably, later, there was a knock on our door. I then learnt that her name was Jennie and after a few cocktails Mountain had her naked on the bed. I honestly couldn't believe my eyes but it was all happening for real. We ended up having some fun and games and later that week she came out to the golf tournament and hung out with us all week long in her time off.

Once the tournament started Richard couldn't get anything going as for some reason he struggled on the greens. Come Sunday we missed a card on the big PGA Tour by a whisker and this was a bitter pill to swallow. All year he had played so well and when it really counted he came up short. It was really sad.

We at least had Pebble Beach to look forward to the next year so we parted company for the off period.

Back in Lawrence the snow fell big time that year and it was really freezing cold. I still couldn't digest just how close we had come to getting on the big PGA Tour and a few more birdies back in Dothan, Alabama would have got us there.

*   *   *

The day I finally arrived at Pebble Beach I knew that I was now going to be on the same stage as the world's best golfers and caddies. I had travelled a long and very interesting road since leaving the clinic in Kansas and this was the cherry on the cake. Richard had his family come over from Wales and I stayed with them as he had rented two nice and expensive apartments close by for the week.

The day I walked on to the practice range for the first time, I soon saw Tiger Woods blasting balls, and finding an open practice spot next to Sergio Garcia I put Richard's big Cleveland bag down. Looking around I realised I was now on golf's biggest stage and how crazy was that. This tournament included celebrities from all over the world. Movie stars, TV stars and well known sports stars all attended this tournament. It was really a world of the who's who and there I stood amongst all of them. I knew people back home wouldn't believe this if I told them. I was finding it hard to believe despite physically being there.

The day after arriving at Pebble Beach Richard got sick and he had to go to bed unsure if he could play that week. After all the excitement and anticipation of getting here this was bad news. Here you had three golf courses to play and we did not know anything about them apart from what we'd seen on television. The usual practice rounds were now out of the question, so it was down to me to figure them out. I then decided on a short cut to check out all the courses by jumping into a golf cart so I could drive around them quickly.

Finally the tournament started and playing Spyglass in the first round, still sick and feeling extremely rough, Richard got everybody talking by shooting an incredible 66 on this tough golf course he had never seen before. Richard was playing with two big American TV stars, Ray Romano and Kevin James and big crowds had followed all day trying to get autographs from these guys.

That night Richard's family praised me for having done a great job. Little did I know the next evening they would be shitting all over me for doing a really bad one.

The second day we played Poppy Hills and arriving on the 14th tee box a caddie's worst nightmare came true. To make things worse Richard was tied for the lead by then. Looking at this hole I realised I had no clue how to play it and taking a total guess I sent Richard in the wrong direction and not even the yardages book could help me out. It turned out to be a dogleg left and I had told him it was a dogleg right.

He obviously went nuts and this all ended up in a double bogey. This only happened because I had driven around on a golf cart not doing my job properly. There was no excuse and I looked like a total fool out there. Everybody was on my case and I couldn't believe he did not fire me right there and then. This obviously rattled him and he lost his momentum dropping down the leaderboard a little. This fuck up would cost him many thousands of dollars too. It was honestly the worst experience in all my years on the golf tours and it all resulted from me being fucking lazy.

Come Sunday, playing Pebble Beach, Richard didn't finish as high up the field as he deserved to, and I had ruined the whole tournament.

I worked for him the rest of the year having moderate success, with a few good results but once again, no PGA Tour card come the end of the season.

*   *   *

Some incidents hurt when you passionately want your man to succeed. I would feel this pain some years later when on Richard's bag and working the final stage of the 2005 Qualifying School in Florida. This had to be the toughest point of all my caddying experiences. Q-School was the gateway to the big time and the PGA Golf Tour, and due to this, it was a big deal for both the golfers and the caddies. A good result at the final stage of Q-School changed people's lives so this was a tense and pressure packed six rounds of golf with big stakes. In my travels I worked the Q-Schools many times going to all the different stages. Starting out, thousands of golfers played the different stages and finally only the best survived to play the final one. Here only a select few would eventually get to play on a major golf tour stage - that's the top 30 players plus ties. The years I worked for Richard Johnson we had made it to the final stage a few times but the one year I actually found myself standing on the 18th hole with tears in my eyes.

As I have said the pressure at the final stage of Q-School is so intense, especially coming down the last few holes when the golfer is close to making the number to advance to the major golf tour. This particular year, playing the final stage in Florida alternating between the Panther Lake and Crooked Cat courses, Richard had played good golf for five rounds and going into the last round he had a great chance of getting the PGA Tour card. On the last nine holes he kicked it into gear making a few birdies and on the 18th Richard had a putt to take our score to 11 under.

Richard stood over the ball, went through his routine and stroked the ball with a control that belied the nerves that surely must have been raging. Left to right break, downhill and down-grain across 18 feet of slick Bermuda grass. The ball turned over smoothly, took the line we'd called and looked to be heading for the hole. Agonisingly the ball slowed and halted, at most a half inch from the middle of the cup. I could have cried. That said, walking off the last hole I was convinced that his 422 total standing at 10 under par would still be good enough to clinch one of the 30 spots.

Arriving in the clubhouse we then discovered that Richard was just inside the magic number and his score looked good enough to get us onto the PGA Tour. There were only a few golfers still on the golf course that could maybe change things, but for most part his score looked safe enough.

If you took all the practice rounds plus the six rounds of golf this was a long and exhausting tournament and basically survival of the fittest in many respects. During the tournament Richard and I had stayed in a hotel nearby and in the evenings hanging out there was always a little tension in the air as we knew how high the stakes really were and why we were there.

Finally, as shit happens in this unpredictable game, a guy called Brett Wetterich unbelievably holed his chip shot on the last hole to knock the guys at 10 under par out to set the magic number at 11 under par. Standing there I was speechless realizing over six rounds of golf just one fucking shot had ruined our dreams, and then the tears came. I know just how big a disappointment this was for me so I could only imagine how Richard must have felt. This guy had played his heart out for six days and finally one shot ended his dream.

The 2005 Q-School saw JB Holmes top the final leaderboard, with D.A Points, Nick Watney and Hunter Mahan amongst the qualifiers. Rare air indeed. In addition to Richard, some other notable names not securing their card were Steve Stricker (423), Scott Hend (423), Boo Weekley (430), Deanne Pappas (430) for whom I had already caddied on the Web.com Tour, Matt Gogel (431) another ex-bag and Jason Dufner (437).

Every year there were the happy and the sad stories at Q-School and this was definitely one of the sad stories. Having come so close to the PGA Tour we all left Florida with heavy hearts to say the least. I had worked for other guys in the past at the Q-Schools so I knew all about the highs and lows but this experience was devastating. Later in my travels on the European Golf Tour I got to work the different stages of Q-School in Europe but I never experienced a close call like this ever again.

Fifteen

This time I spent the off period in Phoenix Arizona as Due North had relocated himself there and what a difference from the snowy freezing times in Lawrence, Kansas. Here you could play golf, walk around in shorts and it was a pleasure being there. I knew that Arizona was hot as hell in the summer but at this time the conditions were perfect.

When I went back to the golf tour the next season finally the breakthrough came I had been looking for. Halfway through the tour, after bouncing around between golfers and having nearly won again with a guy called Jerry Smith, and losing out in a play-off, I picked up the bag of a guy from New Zealand called Michael Long. This guy was high up on the money list and after a few good tournaments come the end of the year he got his prized PGA Tour card. At long last I was finally off to the big PGA Tour and then things came crashing down when he told me he was bringing over a caddie from New Zealand. This arrangement however did not work out too well and he called me to join him on the PGA Tour a little later on. I was now finally a PGA Tour caddie.

I flew out to Pennsylvania to join him and the first week on the PGA Tour I noticed that this guy had changed, as he was short tempered and not as patient as he used to be. Our first tournament together on the PGA Tour he played really well, closing with a 66 on Sunday to make a huge check and it was my biggest payday by far. So there I was, working with the best in the business, living it up and it was the big time for me. I had found the Promised Land and huge crowds turned out as Tiger Woods was always playing and this was a different world, but I knew that having been at Pebble Beach.

The next week at Hartford in Connecticut a freak accident put a major spoke in our wheels and for the next few tournaments Long was out of action. Trying to hit trick shots playing the fool on the practice range, Long pulled a muscle, putting him out of action. He paid me my weekly salary while he recovered and when he was ready to play again he really struggled, throwing temper tantrums out on the golf course. I worked for him a few more tournaments making a few cuts but it was all becoming very stressful for me, not knowing when the guy would boil over.

I was now flying all across America living well but I wasn't having much fun out on the golf course.

When the Tour got to Tampa Bay for a tournament I realised that I had had enough of this stress and I had been so much happier working on the smaller Web.com Tour. The pressure on the PGA Tour was intense as the prize money was so big and everybody seemed on edge. Missing the cut in Tampa Bay I had made up my mind, so I told Long I was done and that I was going to head back to the smaller tour. For so long I had struggled and strived to get on the big tour and when it finally happened it was unfortunately with the wrong golfer and not a very pleasant experience. Spending countless hours each day with the golfer it was tough as there was always tension and stress, but through it all it could be a lot of fun working for a nice relaxed guy like Richard Johnson.

Arriving back, the guys couldn't believe I had given up a job on the PGA Tour but I knew it was the right move considering the circumstances.

Sixteen

Back on the Web.com Tour I had hooked up with a caddie called Thomas with whom I was a good friend and we travelled together. Soon after this, I hooked Thomas up with a player who was a good buddy of one of my previous bosses. Long story short, they really clicked out on the course and went on to win a tournament together.

Arriving in Chattanooga Tennessee I told Thomas he owed me a favour as I helped him win his first tournament, and one night I called the escort service. Two pretty girls arrived at our hotel. I told Thomas he was paying the bill and one of the girls called herself Montanna. She was really stunning and a lot of fun. I told Thomas we would see her again one day.

Not long after this tournament we had a week off and I told Thomas we were going to Chicago for some fun and games. I knew that the PGA tour was having a tournament in Chicago that week and I had a plan up my sleeve.

Arriving in Chicago we went to a big hotel and casino complex. Knowing exactly how casinos operated I asked to see the casino manager.

When a guy in a fancy black suit appeared Thomas said, "What the fuck are you doing dude?" and I replied, "Watch this shit."

I introduced myself to the casino manager, knowing the success of this mission hinged on my accent and the Titleist golf cap on my head. I then explained to the casino manager that I was from South Africa and I had come to play in the PGA Tour golf tournament that week. I continued to tell him that John Daly was my buddy and if he could possibly get me a good discount on a suite I would invite John and the boys over to play at the tables. Everybody knew about Daly's big gambling and I was positive this guy, being the casino manager, also did. Casinos always had rooms and suites set aside and available for big time gamblers they called "whales" and my plan revolved around this fact. Looking at this guy I knew I had him on the line, then and he said that he would see what he could do.

Once he left Thomas said, "Are you fucking crazy dude," and I replied, "I've got him hook, line and sinker dude."

When the casino manager finally returned he handed me a key and a card saying, "It is a privilege to have you stay with us sir. You are welcome to this suite and it's with our compliments."

Shaking his hand and thanking him, I headed for the lifts with Thomas following saying, "You have to be fucking kidding me dude."

In the lift I looked at the card he had given me and it said, free cocktails when presented at any one of our bars.

"This is nuts dude, that's all I can say," Thomas said finally shaking his head.

Opening the hotel room door we walked in and there, right in the middle of the suite in expensive marble we saw the biggest Jacuzzi I had ever seen. The place was a palace with two bedrooms, a fully stocked bar, a kitchen, two huge bathrooms, a huge balcony, a barbecue outside and that huge marble Jacuzzi in the middle of it all.

"This is totally out of control dude," Thomas said walking around and I replied, "You see that Jacuzzi. We are going to bang Montanna in there all week long."

I told him that we were going to fly Montanna to Chicago for a few days.

"You know what it costs for one night dude. Imagine the price for this," Thomas replied and laughing I said, "Buddy, it's not going to cost anything, trust me."

I then continued to call Montanna as we had kept her number from a few weeks earlier. When she decided to answer I said, "Can you get away for a few days and fly to Chicago to come and hang out with Thomas and myself. We won't discuss any money but when we drop you off at the airport I will give you an envelope and let's leave it at that, OK."

She was surprised to hear from me and sounded keen saying she would see what she could arrange and call me back.

"Now I'm convinced you are fucking crazy," Thomas said bursting out in laughter and I replied, "This whole thing is only going to cost a return ticket to Chicago."

The next afternoon Thomas and I picked Montanna up from the airport, as she had to drive to Knoxville to fly out of there. Back at the hotel her eyes lit up when she walked into the suite and she said, "My God you guys are the high rollers aren't you."

That night we treated her to a great meal in the best restaurant in the complex and later in the casino we gave her some money to gamble with. Sitting there I saw the casino manager walking our way so I quickly pulled out a thick wad of dollars cashing it in for chips.

I had to look the part at least when he pitched up and greeting us he said, "I trust your accommodation meets your approval sir," and I replied, "Why don't you ask the lady my friend?"

Smiling, Montanna said, "It's absolutely stunning," and once he had left I had cashed all the chips back into dollars, or most of them anyway.

Montanna seemed to have a good time actually winning some money and going back upstairs we all jumped into the Jacuzzi and the party was on, with room service delivering two bottles of champagne. The next day we took Montanna sightseeing in Chicago and for a few days we partied big time in the hotel and Jacuzzi. The day she left I went to the reception desk and asking for a big envelope I stuffed it with toilet paper and wrote "Montanna" on the envelope. With the toilet paper I enclosed a note saying, "This might help if you cry," and kissing her goodbye at the airport I handed her the big envelope.

Driving away Thomas said, "Shit dude, she is going to freak out," and I replied, "How many guys do you think she has taken for ride my man. It's what she does."

Back on the golf tour Thomas told everybody this crazy story and guys couldn't believe we had actually pulled it all off. I had to admit that I had lost some cash in the casino so it wasn't all totally on the house, but still a great deal no doubt as that suite had to cost thousands of dollars we thought, plus the free entertainment.

*   *   *

When the Tour ended that season I decided to go to Las Vegas for a visit, and spending a week there it was hookers, drinking and non-stop gambling. Eventually, in a drunken stupor, I realised that I had lost just about all my money and I was in trouble. I had made good money from the golf that year but in a few days I had lost it all in Las Vegas and I was basically stranded. The only plan I could think of was to finally return to South Africa. I then called my brother, or half-brother as we had the same mother but different fathers, and asked him to help me get a ticket back to Johannesburg.

My days in America were now finally over and I knew I had overstayed my welcome anyway. It had all been an awesome roller-coaster ride but it was over and I knew with all my experience I could get hired on the European Golf Tour. I had been around America many times and travelling in Europe would be an opportunity to see the rest of the world. I realised I was down but not out, and going back to South Africa was only a stepping stone to getting on the European Tour. In Europe I could at least work legally and knowing by now travelling was my thing, it all made sense.

I had been away for quite a few years and it was time to move on and experience different things. Up until then I had been pushing my luck and maybe losing all my money was the wake-up call that I needed to change direction.

Open Bag

Pierre Van Achterbergh

Pierre Van Achterbergh - PGA and European Tour, multi-event winning, professional caddie.

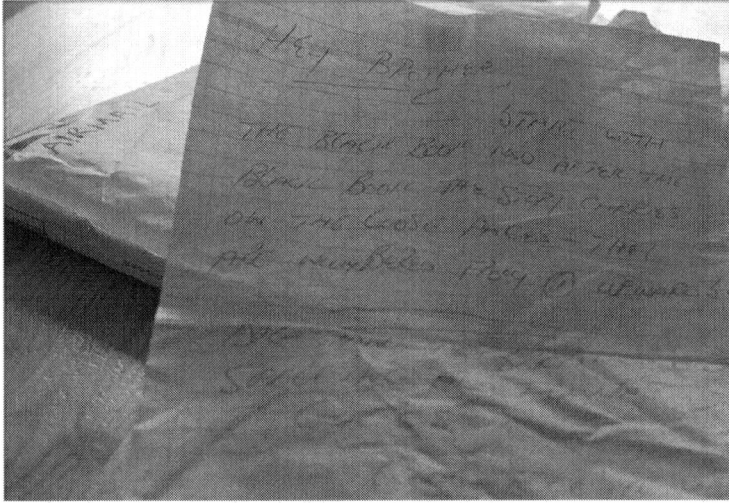

"Hey Brother". The tattered letter in which Pierre reaches out to Rob Johnson, brother of Richard, seeking help with telling his story in a bid to escape the streets of Durban.

The warm informal address gives an insight to the familial relationship borne from sincere endeavour inside the ropes during seasons long since past.

The feint and margin notebook mailed to Robert, continuing on loose pages and the back of airline booking sheets, that evidence a life once filled with international travel.

Pierre Van Achterbergh

Pierre sitting at the Nomads Backpackers committing his story, without computer, to a feint and margin notebook.

Pierre with fellow caddie and great friend, Due North.

Front view of the caddie bib worn for Richard Johnson at the 2001 AT&T National Pro-Am at Pebble Beach.

Rear view of the caddie bib worn for Richard Johnson at the 2001 AT&T National Pro-Am at Pebble Beach.

Final round of the 2008 French Open, Alstom with Pablo Larrazabal. Pablo would shoot 67 to win by 4 shots over Colin Montgomerie.

At a Durban beach having returned to South Africa.

Seventeen

The day that I arrived back in South Africa, my two sisters met me at the airport and it was great seeing them again, it had been years and it made me realise how much I'd missed them. That night we had a family get together and I sat there telling them all about my travels. They were concerned about my future but I explained that I was an experienced golf caddie and my services would always be in demand somewhere.

Back in South Africa I played some golf and I was staying with my brother and his family, really just hanging out deciding on my next move in life. America was now a closed chapter and going to Europe was top of my To-Do list. In America I had met a golfer called Steve Alker and he had told me that he was going to go and play on the European Golf Tour. Remembering this, I decided to contact him and find out what he was doing. The funny thing was that the European Golf Tour actually had a few tournaments in South Africa at the beginning of the season, which were combined with the local South African Sunshine Tour.

After some detective work I finally got hold of Steve Alker again and he informed me that he was in fact coming to play in South Africa. Amazingly the chips all seemed to fall perfectly into place for me, as he hired me to caddie for him on the European Tour. All the pieces of the puzzle now fitted perfectly and my family were surprised how quickly I had arranged things.

The first tournament that I picked up Alker's bag was the Joburg Open in Johannesburg. Now I got to meet a whole new lot of people and caddies but it was all the same stuff going on day in day out. The only big difference here was you had people from many different countries all speaking different languages. Alker was a really nice guy and easy to work for. I had to pinch myself as there I was, working on the European Golf Tour.

That week we missed the cut by one shot and next we were going to Jakarta in Indonesia. This was pretty exciting stuff as now the rest of the world was about to open up to me, and I was on my way to see and experience it. I did now however face another problem. Being a South African, I needed all sorts of visas to travel, and arranging these was a huge pain in the arse. Starting out travelling on this tour I was on my own so I had to try and figure shit out myself and it was all totally different to running around America. Nearly every country that you visit across Europe requires paperwork.

*　　*　　*

Arriving in Jakarta it was the early hours of the morning and standing outside the airport, there were many shady looking characters hanging around. Grabbing the first taxi I saw, I jumped in as I had located some sort of hotel near the golf course on the Internet. My brother had financed my start on the European Tour but I was on a very tight budget for sure. As we were driving along the sun came up and then all hell broke loose it seemed. Old battered cars and scooters appeared, thousands of them from nowhere and it was just total chaos everywhere. The traffic was out of control and going to the hotel there were horns honking non-stop as we weaved our way through narrow crowded streets. On the sidewalks people were cooking food and flea market type stalls littered the pavements. This was all so crazy having just travelled America, and not to mention the crowds of people hustling and bustling around.

Arriving at the hotel I was just happy and relieved to be in one piece. It didn't take long to figure out that this was no five star hotel, a far cry from the hotel suite myself and Thomas shared in Chicago. The place was dark, very bare and basic. The room consisted of a hard bed with an old set of table and chairs. From down below in the street, strange food smells wafted up through the small window I had opened. The noise was loud and it was all pretty different to anything I had seen before. The shower and toilet was located in the hallway and it was honestly bare and basic living here. I jumped into the shower and freshened up. Walking out later into the street, what felt like a heatwave nearly knocked me over. It was boiling hot and very humid out there and I knew it was going to be hell out on the golf course.

Walking around I saw some strange things but I soon realized that many of the girls here were very pretty with dark smooth skin. They were also very small and petite. As for me, I just seemed to have people staring at me the whole time. Being a white man in this city, I stood out like a sore thumb. I saw some weird and crazy things being cooked in huge pots on the pavements and it was a different world to the one I was used to, but also very fascinating. Finding some sort of pavement café, I sat down and ordered what looked like eggs from a very tatty and torn menu with an orange juice to go with them. When the food arrived it was very tasty to say the least, they had scrambled the eggs with some green veggies of sorts, peppers and onions. It was all dirt cheap and sitting there watching the passing parade I saw a lot of these small pretty girls staring at me. I also knew it wasn't going to take too long before I unwrapped one of these Asian delights.

Back at the hotel I knew that I had to go and check out the golf course. Being on this tour now, all the golf courses were going to be new to me, and a lot of extra work was going to be required. I always thought back to my horrible experience earlier in my career with Richard, I had learnt my lesson by then and getting to know all the courses was a top priority. In Johannesburg I had played the two golf courses used for that tournament a hundred times before, but now it was going to be a different story. Hopping on a three wheel tuk tuk taxi scooter, I had a wild ride to the golf course causing me to sweat my arse off.

In America all of the caddies had spent time living and travelling together but in Europe it was all a different game. Guys travelled pretty much alone and they stayed spread out all over the place. As I say, you had guys from so many different countries all speaking different languages and the different nationalities seemed to stick together. I did a good job walking the golf course in the sweltering heat and never ever was another Poppy Hills drama going to happen to me. When Steve Alker arrived I knew the golf course inside out and he was impressed that I had done my homework.

*　　*　　*

One evening whilst sitting on the patio having a few beers at the hotel, I asked a waiter who spoke some broken English where the best place was to find some girls. Hearing this, he then said that he had a very pretty cousin who would love to come to the hotel and join me for cocktails and dinner, but it would cost me some money. Within ten minutes of the discussion I'd had with the waiter, a loud and smoking scooter pulled up with two people on it. When the girl sitting on the back took her helmet off I couldn't believe my eyes. The waiter's cousin was smoking with long black hair, all these girls had black hair but she was beautiful. The waiter then introduced her to me but she didn't speak any English. It was all very strange really, as here I had this pretty petite girl sat in front of me and we couldn't have any conversation. The waiter brought her some fancy cocktail with a piece of fruit and a little umbrella, and we sat there just looking at each other.

In the restaurant we managed to get something going as she pointed out things on the menu giving the thumbs up sign. I let her order and giggling she ordered another cocktail. When the food arrived it was like a mountain of noodles with different meats all cooked in with great tasting spicy sauces. We used broken sign language to get through the huge meal, but later back in the hotel room this little Asian girl took complete control of things. She undressed me giving me a good massage and this had to be heaven on earth I thought. She knew all the tricks in the book and when she left I was exhausted. I knew from then on, Asian girls had shot to the top of my ladies list.

*   *   *

That week Alker came to play, and come Friday we made the cut easily. On this tour I now saw many famous golfers I had seen on TV before, and it was large crowds and TV cameras everywhere just like the PGA Tour. The European Tour was also big with large prize money on offer and many of the world's top golfers played there.

During the week the Asian girl came back a few times and everything was so much better than America I thought. It definitely was a lot more exciting and fun.

Come Sunday Alker had played good golf to finish in the top twenty, so I had some cash back in my pocket again. I knew that between my sessions at the hotel with Miss Asia and all the rounds of golf in a hundred degrees I had definitely lost some weight that week too.

Eighteen

From here, my travels then took me to Spain and what a blast it was travelling there. I loved Spain and everything about it especially the tapas bars. Here you could hang out sampling different foods and sipping good wine. Spain over the next few years would become one of my favourite hangout spots. I loved everything that it had to offer. Europe also had the most awesome old buildings and so much history. On this tour the whole scene changed every week as it was different languages, different cultures, different food, different people, sometimes different money and what an experience this all was.

During my days working for Steve Alker on the European Tour, one of the most memorable incidents happened on the Golf course that ended up sending, you could say shock waves through the golfing world, at least on the European Tour anyway. Going to the Moscow Open in early August 2007 at Le Meridien on the European Tour, Steve Alker and I stayed together sharing a room. This whole tournament turned out to be a fun deal as the Russians made a huge effort to provide top class entertainment and hospitality for both golfers and caddies. We all stayed in a very fancy hotel as the tournament was played at a resort just outside Moscow. As it turned out my man Alker missed the cut come Friday, and he left Russia leaving me on my own in the fancy hotel room.

During the week I had met a South African Golfer called Dawie Van Der Walt who had been invited to play in this tournament and we clicked from the get go and became buddies. This guy had been playing well Thursday and Friday, and as my man had missed the cut I asked Van Der Walt if he wanted me to caddie for him on the Saturday and Sunday. On both the PGA Tour in America and the European Tour all the golfers had to have a caddie to carry their bags. However that week in Russia there were not enough caddies and the rule was changed so some of the golfers were using push carts themselves. Van Der Walt had pushed his own cart for the first two rounds so being in the hunt on the weekend I reckoned that he now needed a caddie so that's why I asked him. As it then turned out I caddied for him on Saturday and Sunday and he also took Alker's place by moving into the hotel room with me.

On Saturday Van Der Walt played great golf jumping onto the leaderboard finding himself all over the TV that day, all the cameras were following us around. After the round finished I saw that we were near the top of the leaderboard, but I also noticed that that the leaderboard had our score one shot better than it actually was. I couldn't figure this out and suspected that the score had been posted incorrectly.

On the Sunday I spoke to Van Der Walt about this and after quickly going back through the round shot-by-shot myself, I believed we had shot 69. I felt that something was amiss and if we had in fact signed a wrong score card it would likely mean instant disqualification from the tournament. Anyway, we continued to play and staying on the leaderboard, Van Der Walt completed with a 4th place finish and made a huge cheque, some € 73,000 and change.

Remaining uneasy some days after the Sunday prize giving that the total score was wrong by one shot due to the 68 posted on Saturday I decided to contact the European Tour officials to talk the matter through with them.

Van Der Walt met the officials and the discrepancy between the 68 on the scorecard, and the 69 actually shot was clarified. An amendment was made resulting in the award of a disqualification and the money list adjusted accordingly.

This all happened more than a week after the tournament was finished. The European Tour director of operations David Garland explained later that Van Der Walt had signed for a four on the 13th, where he took a five, and even though the tournament was completed he had still been disqualified under Rule 34-1b III; "returned a score for any hole lower than actually taken for any reason other than failure to include a penalty that, before the competition closed, he did not know he had incurred".

Further, Garland explained that due to the lateness of discovering the error, Van Der Walt would not have to give up the entry place at the Scandinavian Masters that had been earned with the top ten finish, nor any winnings from the event. Van Der Walt had gone on to secure a five-over 43rd place finish for a further € 8,000.

It is unfortunate to have this sort of incident at any level of our game, let alone on a professional Tour. It all was really crazy as I was the only one who had picked this up, though I was pleased to receive a letter from the European Tour thanking me for my honesty and integrity.

Nineteen

Amsterdam was the next stop and arriving in Holland, I was to hit the big time in this world of professional golf once again. Amsterdam was such a cool city and I loved the crazy place. Everybody was so laid back, hanging out, getting stoned, sitting in sidewalk cafes just drinking and mellowing out. The red light district was fascinating with all sorts of girls sitting behind big windows flashing their boobs. People just strolled around having a good time. After a few beers I walked past a stunning blonde girl sitting behind one of these windows and I couldn't resist the temptation, so I went in.

Leaving Amsterdam I headed to Zandvoort, home of the KLM Airlines Dutch Open golf tournament. Once again I had to go check out the golf course and many big name golfers were playing here this week. Being from South Africa I could understand the Dutch people and make conversation with them. Staying in a nice bed and breakfast owned by an older lady I chatted to her without a problem. I could see that this lady had been a hottie in her younger days and even then she was still in decent shape.

Once the tournament started the Dutch crowds turned up in their thousands and my man Alker got his act together popping onto the leaderboard. Come Friday his name was still on the leaderboard and here I was in the mix on the European Tour again.

Zandvoort was a beautiful town located by the sea and the Friday night I invited my host, the older lady to join me for dinner. She lived on her own in one of the rooms and the rest of her house was the bed and breakfast. We found a great restaurant on the waterfront and spent a lovely evening chatting in Dutch and Afrikaans, which were very similar languages. After two bottles of wine I could see this lady was tipsy and later, walking home she had to use my arm to steady herself. Finally I put my arm around her and guided her home and arriving there she wouldn't let go of me driving me upstairs to her room.

Once in her room I thought my job was done and I would leave but she started to kiss me. Being a gentleman, I had to obey the lady's wishes. When they say many a good tune is played on an old fiddle, believe it. I guessed this lady had not had sex for years but she seemed determined to make up for it all that night.

On Saturday I arrived at the golf course, a little hung over with love bites all over my throat and some caddies said, "Oh, too much of the Dutch or what?"

* * *

I knew we were going to be on TV that day as Alker was on the leaderboard and back in South Africa people I knew were going to be watching us. Out on the golf course we had huge crowds following us along with the TV cameras. Alker climbed higher up the leaderboard. There I was in the thick of things on the European Tour with a guy trying to win this the tournament. This was the top of the golfing ladder, having a good shot at winning on one of the world's major golf tours.

Walking on to the 18th green the large crowd was on its feet cheering Steve Alker as his name stood right at the top of the leaderboard. We were going to be leading the Dutch Open going into the last round on Sunday.

That night my host the older lady seemed very shy and I guess embarrassed as she apologised to me for her out of character behaviour the previous evening.

I then kissed her on the forehead saying, "Dit was baie lekker moenie worry nie." This English meant, "Don't worry, it was very nice."

Come Sunday it was the biggest day in my caddie life as we were playing in the last group with Ross Fisher, with a real chance of winning this tournament. At the golf course it was madness with big crowds and TV people all around us. People were trying to get autographs and there was some pretty tense and nerve-wracking stuff going on. On the very first hole I knew we were totally out gunned and playing for second place. Having been around this game as long as I had, you sometimes just knew certain things.

This guy Ross Fisher hit the ball miles and my man Alker was short off the tee box. Fisher's ball was so far ahead of us and I knew that he was hitting easy scoring clubs into the greens. Alker was hitting a 5 iron and Fisher maybe an 8 or 9 iron. I honestly knew we had no chance of beating this guy but my man Alker was grinding away trying his best.

Fisher played some great golf that day and after a tense day out on the golf course we walked on to the 18th green with the crowd cheering the champion, Ross Fisher. My man Alker had put up a brave fight and finishing in third place he had done really well, making a big cheque for our efforts. I had now also earned some big money too as I received seven percent of Alker's prize money. This had been a great experience to be part of and I knew this was what made everything worth it in the end.

* * *

Leaving Holland we were on our way to Switzerland and here I was to discover maybe the most beautiful country in the whole world. We flew into Geneva and took the train that ran along the big lake and what amazing scenery this was. We then went up into the snow covered mountains to a town called Crans Montana. This was no doubt God's country, high up in the mountains with the clouds actually floating around down below us in the valleys.

When I met Alker at the golf course he handed me a brown paper bag and opening it my eyes nearly popped out of my head.

It was stacked full of English pounds and he said, "That's your share of the prize money from Holland."

This was nuts as normally the golfers transferred caddie payments into their bank accounts but Alker had paid me cash. Here I was, walking around with a paper bag stuffed full of British pounds. It was crazy. Alker had won euros in Holland but he had paid me in pounds so no problem, but in cold hard cash, that was a problem.

Leaving the golf course I took a casual walk back to the hotel up a steep hill and lo and behold what appeared in front, of all things in this world, a fucking casino. Here up in the mountains, covered in snow, I'm walking along and I discover a casino and I have thousands of pounds stuffed in a brown paper bag. What could possibly be worse than that? I was honestly like a moth drawn to a flame, I changed direction and walked straight towards the casino.

*   *   *

In the Crans Montana casino I saw a few guys I had met in my travels and I changed some of the pounds into Swiss money. Before I knew it I was at the roulette table placing absolute heaps of chips all over the table ordering drink after drink.

By the time I left the casino the brown paper bag had shrunk by at least half, and I knew I had lost a serious amount of money. This gambling thing literally had me by the balls and every time I found myself in shit, gambling was responsible for it. I actually felt sick to my stomach walking back to my hotel knowing what gambling had always done to me.

*   *   *

That week the fireworks on the golf course seemed to have vanished as Alker amazingly missed the cut. Friday night I found myself back in the casino eventually losing the rest of the pounds. I had actually lost thousands of pounds that week and it really was a very sad state of affairs, but somehow I couldn't fucking help myself.

Leaving this beautiful country I had a bad taste in the mouth and I was on my way to Portugal. Arriving in Lisbon I made my way to Estoril and here I found another amazing place by the sea. There were great restaurants and bars everywhere and here I got to eat the best chicken in the world. In this country they made the famous Portugese Peri Peri chicken and it was the real thing for sure.

Once again back on the golf course things didn't get any better and it was hard to believe that two weeks ago my man had nearly won a tournament. The competition out here was obviously very strong so these professionals had to produce the goods in order to achieve results and some weeks this happened but some weeks it didn't I guess.

By now I had come across a caddie from New Zealand called Roger, who I had met in America and this was great as he helped me get around as he had travelled through Europe many times before. We also shared a double room pretty often and this guy liked to hang out in the pubs and drink the nights away as I did.

Alker had also qualified to play in the British Open so I got to caddie in what I believe is the world's biggest tournament at Carnoustie, Scotland. What an experience this was. Here I got to hang out and work with the very best in the world of golf but we sadly never made the cut. After this I travelled to many more countries but nothing good was happening on the golf courses. When the golf season ended, Steve Alker had not managed to keep his European Tour card. At the end of the golf season only the top 110 golfers on the money list got to keep their European Tour cards to play on the tour again the following year. The rest of the players then had to go to the European Qualifying School to try and qualify to get back there.

Twenty

Arriving back in South Africa I didn't have a job on the Tour anymore and the New Year wasn't looking too good. My brother and his family went on holiday and I looked after their house wondering how I was ever going to get back on the golf tour again. Finding golfers to caddie for on this tour was the same as it was in America. Very difficult and virtually impossible to do.

When the new golf season arrived the European Tour started in South Africa and there I was, in South Africa without a job, it was so frustrating.

One afternoon my phone rang and a caddie called John I knew was calling from Ireland. He told me that he was working for a young Spanish golfer called Pablo Larrazabal and that this guy was playing in South Africa. John explained that he couldn't come to South Africa and asked me if I could caddie for his man Larrazabal in the tournament to help him out. I obviously grabbed this opportunity so at least I was working again. Once I arrived at the Joburg Open once again, I met the Spanish guy and he was really lively and funny. He also spoke English pretty well too. It was fun working for this guy and he could play some golf. He was a young guy and a rookie on the Tour and nobody really knew anything about him.

After the first two rounds I knew that people were going to hear a lot about this kid as he had all the shots and we made the cut easily. On Saturday he got it going, making birdies and his name jumped onto the leaderboard. Finally standing on the 18th green this guy nobody knew was leading the golf tournament. My brother and family were really excited and they were coming to the tournament the next day to support us.

Once again I had a chance to caddie for a guy who could win, and this was great after all the bad tournaments I had experienced in Europe the previous season after the KLM tournament.

Sunday it was the same madness with crowds and TV crews and I wondered if this kid could hang in under all the pressure. Being a rookie on the tour I knew after Holland how much pressure this kid was going to be under leading this tournament. Out on the golf course I could see that the kid was a little nervous and he hit some bad shots dropping down the leaderboard. I knew he had obviously never been in this position before and the pressure finally got to him.

Finally playing the 18th hole, a par 5, Larrazabal needed a birdie to finish in the top five at least. Crushing a drive here he only had a 4 iron into the green. He missed the green with his approach to the right, landing in a greenside bunker. He played a good bunker shot leaving himself maybe a 6 foot putt for birdie. Here the nerves really got the kid as he unbelievably three putted and spent thousands of euros in the process. I honestly felt sorry for this nice guy but I also knew he had learned some valuable lessons that day and that he would be back in this position again, leading a tournament very soon.

The next time John the caddie called me he told me that he was now going to work for another player, so I could call Larrazabal and ask him if I could work for him permanently. So next thing I knew I was employed by the Spanish kid and off to Europe again, not even dreaming that this kid and I were about to set the golfing world on fire.

*   *   *

In Ireland at the Irish Open he came alive, having a chance to win, but didn't quite manage it. He did however, manage to finish on the leaderboard once again. This was the dream job as this kid could play and we had a great time working together. We quickly became friends both on and off the course.

Twenty One

We soon found ourselves on a short break, so I joined another caddie Roachie on a trip to Thailand as some of the other caddies lived there. I soon fell in love with this place and this was a country I wanted to live in. The people were friendly, great food, it was really cheap and the girls were pretty. I had developed a liking for Asian girls and here you could pick and choose and some nights I ended up with two or three young girls. If you had some cash you could live like a king here amongst all these pretty girls.

One day, going to have my eyes tested, I met this young beautiful girl called Ta who was the optometrist and taking her out to dinner that night things happened. By the time I left Thailand I had rented a nice apartment and she had moved in with me. I planned to spend all my off time in Thailand and Ta would continue to live at the apartment. I sent her the rent money every month, and for the first time in ages I had a steady girlfriend of sorts and she was fun to be around. We had chatted about her starting her own business and I told her if I made some big money on the golf tour I would help her.

The town I had set up the apartment in was called "Pattaya" located on the sea about 2 hours drive from Bangkok. The apartment was on the first floor of a tall block. Suffering from claustrophobia I couldn't ride in a elevator at the best of times so the first floor suited me just fine. I spent some cash sorting the apartment out with a huge TV, sound system and many other things. It ended up a real luxury pad. The apartment was close to the famous Walking Street so it was always busy with people hanging out in bars and restaurants. I basically found myself right in the middle of the Devils Den with bars and hookers everywhere. Walking out of the apartment down a flight of stairs you found yourself on a very busy street with all sorts of things going on. The thing I enjoyed the most was all the great food you could find at the various sidewalk kitchens. One lady would have different noodles in her pan and the guy next to her had all sorts of great smelling kebabs cooking on a fire. This was how it went all the way down the street. This place was great value for money and a tourist hot spot. I honestly lived like a king with all sorts of money to throw around. Flying in and out of Bangkok was easy enough so now I had a base to work from whilst caddying in Europe and Asia.

* * *

Back caddying in Europe, Larrazabal and I had a few average tournaments making most of the cuts, and going to France for a tournament in St Omer the kid had told me that he was going to try and qualify for the French Open. The French Open was one of the biggest tournaments on the golf tour with four million euros in prize money. Larrazabal was not in this tournament as the world's best golfers played here and he was not ranked high enough. However, there was a Monday qualifying tournament for the French Open with six spots available. Nearly all of the players that weren't ranked high enough tried to qualify for one of these coveted spots.

During the St Omer tournament Pablo got a bad case of the flu and they had to drive him off the golf course in a golf cart to see a doctor. The following Monday was the qualifying for the French Open which consisted of thirty six holes of golf. I drove the rental car to a small town near the qualifying golf course and got Pablo into bed giving him all sorts of flu and cold medication.

Come Monday the guy was still feeling bad but he bravely got out of bed to play golf. By this time I knew what this guy was capable of on the course, so I was by no means surprised when he blew everybody away to win the qualifying tournament, shooting ten under par for the two rounds. So now we were playing in the French Open in Paris and for some reason I had a funny feeling about things.

*   *   *

Arriving in Paris this tournament was big news. Lee Westwood and Colin Montgomerie were just two of the many big stars in the field.

During the practice round I realised this course was very hard and dry and the ball was running forever on the fairways. After the round I took the driver out of Larrazabal's bag telling him that he wasn't going to use it during the tournament.

He was surprised to say the least, and looking at me he said "I've never played without a driver," and I replied, "Well you are going to this week."

His three wood was long and with the hard course more than enough, and this wood would keep the ball in play. On Thursday this young Spanish kid once again had the golf world talking by shooting an amazing 65 to lead the French Open. On Friday we played steady to shoot a 70 but he still had the lead and this was big news in Paris. This kid who had to qualify for the tournament was leading and it was all a fairy tale according to the newspapers.

When Saturday arrived the crowds were huge, following this kid and we were all over sports TV that day. Staying calm under all the pressure, the kid played flawless golf to shoot 67 and stay in the lead at the French Open. This was now a really big story combined with the fact that he was playing the monster golf course without a driver. The newspapers were full of the story of the unknown Spanish kid that had to qualify to play in this tournament.

On Sunday it was the same hectic stuff as people had come out in their thousands to see if this young kid could do the impossible and win the French Open.

Colin Montgomerie was also on the leaderboard and the golf channel interviewed him asking, "So what do you think of this Larrazabal kid? Can he win today?" and Monty replied, "Who are you talking about, sorry what is his name?"

I stood listening to this thinking to myself, "This kid is going to kick your arse today and you know exactly who this kid is, as he has been leading this tournament since the very first day."

Back home in South Africa my brother was having a party at his house so they could watch it all on TV and it was all big news. I also knew that not much in this world of professional golf could get bigger than what was happening that day in Paris. Guys won major tournaments sure, but most were well known players, here you had an unknown kid who wasn't in the tournament until the Monday, and here he was trying to win the French Open, one of the biggest tournaments on the European tour.

Starting out the round on Sunday I said to Larrazabal, "OK buddy, let's have some fun and relax out there today. OK?"

This young kid was ready to win, I could just see and feel it that day. He stayed calm and we joked and laughed our way around the golf course. Arriving at the 9th hole, a par 5, Larrazabal was still in the lead and hitting a good drive he wanted to go for the green with his second shot. I agreed with him but he missed the green ending up in a greenside bunker.

Playing the bunker shot, he hit it over the green into some bushes. The crowd gasped and the TV commentator walking with us said, "Oh no folks the young kid is in big trouble here on the 9th hole. The pressure is finally kicking in."

Walking off the green Larrazabal had made a double bogey on this easy hole and he had let a few players back into the picture. Most people thought that finally he was folding under all the pressure, but I knew different and I wasn't very concerned despite the double bogey.

I could also see that he was not rattled by this and standing on the 10th tee box he said, "Forget that mate, let's go."

Hearing this I honestly admired the kid, and with the balls that he had, I knew that he was going to win this tournament.

He then proceeded to birdie both the 10th and 11th holes to go back ahead and as far as I was concerned it was all over, as I knew nobody was going to catch him. Finally standing on the last hole, Larrazabal had a four shot lead and walking onto the 18th green I had goose flesh as the huge crowd stood up to cheer the French Open champion, Pablo Larrazabal from Spain.

This kid had done the impossible and caused the golfing upset of the year. He had led the French Open all the way and beaten many of the world's best without folding under all the pressure. After sinking his last putt for another 67, Larrazabal ran and dived into the water around the green and the crowd went crazy. I stood there holding the flag, realizing I had just become an instant millionaire back home in South African money. My share of the prize money made me a fucking millionaire back home! It was a crazy thought, but true.

I had kids grabbing at me walking back to the clubhouse, wanting my cap and golf balls, it was madness all around. Eventually, after the prize giving ceremony Larrazabal and I arrived in the locker room and looking at each other we burst out laughing because neither us knew what to really say.

Eventually I stood up and hugging this kid I said, "You are a champion my friend. It was an honour and privilege to have walked the golf course with you this week."

Twenty Two

That evening I sat on a ferry leaving France for England with a cold beer knowing my life had changed that day. I now was well set financially and working for a new superstar golfer and I had the world at my feet. Like cream does, I had risen to the very top finally and right then I was no doubt one of the best professional golf caddies in the world. I thought back to that clinic in Kansas City and wondered if Frank Wilson had any idea of what had happened in Paris.

Now a lot of things changed out on the golf tour as Larrazabal had joined the elite group of players. He was going to play in the British Open at Royal Birkdale. He was going to play for Spain in the World Cup with Miguel Jimenez. He was going to play big tournaments in America and basically he was a superstar now.

Arriving at the British Open at Royal Birkdale, Larrazabal and I had our first argument ever as I asked him why I had not been paid my money from the French Open yet. We were talking about a huge amount of money and he said that he did not want to discuss money matters.

Hearing this I said, "What the fuck are you talking about? I work for you so you have to discuss this."

He then said that I had to sort it out with his father who often travelled with him. This was all bullshit as far as I was concerned and finding his father I told him he had to sort the money thing out and very soon. His brother then came to me asking me to sign an invoice for the money they were going to pay me. Looking at this it was for a smaller amount than it should have been and I refused to sign it. Caddies always received ten percent of the total first prize money and that's exactly what I wanted, nothing less.

The brother then went to discuss this with the family and the next day he told me that Pablo had been taxed in France and that's why I was getting less money. I knew this wasn't my problem as caddies always got ten percent of the total amount of the prize money and we argued about this.

Finally I thought, "Fuck these guys," and not at all happy with the situation I signed and got paid the smaller amount.

I then learnt from other caddies that some of the Spanish golfers did this, paying the caddie after the taxes had been deducted. Evidently none of the other golfers did this but it was known to happen amongst Spanish golfers. Despite this I still had a fat bank account now and I started living the high life. It was expensive hotels, high dollar strip clubs, you name it I could afford it.

* * *

At the British Masters he finished on the leaderboard again and then on home soil in Spain at the Madrid Open the fireworks started again. Being Spanish he was a local hero here and big crowds had followed him around. The first two rounds he struggled, finally just making the cut on the number and way back in the field. I guess not having high hopes then we both ended up going out the Friday night drinking and partying until the sun came up. I was in a dance club in Madrid which was a big time party city and Larrazabal was doing the same somewhere else with his buddies.

When I saw this guy on Saturday morning he honestly was still drunk saying, "Seriously mate, I can't play today I'm feeling sick."

I was hung over feeling sick myself and we both looked a sorry sight. I remember this kid couldn't even get his golf shoes on his feet it was that bad. Finally we both burst out laughing in the locker room rolling on the floor with tears running down our faces.

"What the hell?" Pablo kept shouting and we laughed louder and louder.

Eventually standing on the tee box I knew anything was possible out on the golf course that day, expecting this kid to throw up, shooting a million.

Once we got going the whole round of golf sort of took place in a daze believe me. As we went along I noticed the crowd getting larger and larger and then all sorts of TV cameras appeared from nowhere and then I saw a leaderboard with Larrazabal on it. I then returned to reality but Pablo was not saying a word to anybody. I knew this guy was making all sorts of putts but we were honestly completely out of sorts and hung over as all hell. The whole drama unfolding that day has to go down as the biggest miracle ever in professional golf, trust me.

When this hung over Spanish kid sank his last putt on the 18th hole he had a buzz going in the golf world as he had just shot an incredible 62 in the Madrid Open.

He had rocketed to the top of the leaderboard from nowhere and I will never forget him saying to me, "I think I played good today but I'm not sure."

This kid honestly said that and I burst out laughing. This was as crazy as things could get in my book anyway and Pablo was a Spanish hero that day.

Come Sunday it was total chaos at the golf course as this young kid was trying to follow the success at Alstom with a win at his country's national golf tournament. He was playing with South African Charl Schwarzel and the newspapers were shouting about the 62 on Saturday. Obviously what happened Saturday was out of the ordinary but I knew we had a good shot at winning on Sunday.

The whole day was really exciting and finally making a birdie on the 18th hole Larrazabal finished up in third place with the South African winning. So leaving Spain people now knew about this kid, but perhaps not fully anticipating the glittering career that was about to follow.

*　　*　　*

On our way to a tournament in Valderrama we stayed in Madrid and here my wheels were to totally fall off.

One night I went to a very high class strip club with the best looking Russian girls you could imagine. After many drinks I took two tall blond stunning girls to the VIP room ordering bottles of very expensive champagne and these girls produced a little gold box full of cocaine. I was never into any drugs at all but that night I got totally fucked up on champagne and cocaine, banging these girls non-stop, high as a kite. Leaving the place my bill was enormous but I was so high I didn't really care at that stage.

Arriving in Valderrama I was coming down from the drugs and booze and I felt sick and useless. I could hardly get around the golf course and it was all a nightmare happening out there. Having another argument with Larrazabal about something I finally thought, "Fuck it, I needed a holiday."

I then plonked Larrazabal's bag down on the practice range and I told him I no longer was going to caddie for him. This guy couldn't believe what he was hearing but I simply marched off and the next day I was on a flight to Bangkok. I was also burnt out with the golf and I just wanted to get away from it all.

Twenty Three

Arriving in Pattaya I found Ta living comfortably in the apartment and I spent my days on the beach relaxing, and going to good restaurants at night living a very relaxed and care free life at first. Ta then told me that a friend of hers was selling his beach front apartment for a good price and liking it, I bought the place for cash money. So now I owned my own spot in Thailand and we moved in.

I took her on holiday to all kinds of exotic islands and golf was not in the picture for me at that stage. I was enjoying this care free life in Thailand and Ta knew that I was also visiting other girls on the side but as I looked after her she did not say too much about it. I was living like a king with a harem riding a scooter from bar to bar most days along the beachfront, just chilling out and chatting up the girls.

I now had also started to gamble online on my laptop computer and I spent hours gambling on horse racing and I also placed big bets on different sports events. I won often and lost often, and then one week I hit the jackpot. The European Golf Tour was in Qatar and I saw on the sports betting that a player called Alvaro Quiros carried odds of 70-1. I knew this golf course and I knew a guy like Quiros who hit the ball incredibly far could win on this golf course. I then placed a large bet in British pounds as my bank account was with HSBC Bank in England. I bet on Quiros finishing in the top five plus a big bet on him winning the tournament.

Amazingly then as things turned out, this guy did win the tournament and I ended up winning fifty thousand pounds.

Gambling was illegal in Thailand so I gambled on the Internet and it was always an up and down thing, providing the rush that gambling gave me.

I then ran into a visa problem in Thailand and I was having to leave and enter on a regular basis to be there legally. Mostly I made trips to the border leaving and returning the same day but I did make a few trips to other places in Asia. For six months I lived the relaxed holiday life in Thailand and I had been looking around for a business to buy for Ta. I thought a restaurant and bar sounded good but she said a laundry was a good business, washing clothes for all the tourists.

One night I got in over my head with the online gambling by placing three massive bets on football matches in England. One of the bets was on Barcelona playing against a shitty team. Barcelona had not lost a game for a long time and despite bad odds I figured it was stealing money. When the match ended in a draw I couldn't believe it and lost a fortune. I knew nothing in life is a sure thing but this was a real upset. These were really huge bets and I ended up losing all these bets which virtually cleaned out my bank account overnight. All the teams I had backed drew their games and it was really hard to believe, but it happened. Someone once said the only way to double your money is to fold it over and put it back in your pocket. I knew this was true but I kept throwing good money after bad. This was a major disaster and my happy holiday in Thailand had gone up in smoke. Suddenly I was in big trouble and I knew only the golf could save me then.

*　　*　　*

Leaving Thailand I was obviously bitter and twisted but I had dealt with gambling knocks and problems all my life so I guess I was pretty used to it all by then. I also knew that if I did not have the gambling problem I could have been retired if I wanted to with all the money I had made in my life.

Arriving back on the golf tour I encountered a new problem. The word had got out about me dumping Larrazabal at Valderrama and nobody wanted a hire me anymore. So I was both broke and jobless back on the European Tour looking for a bag. When this didn't work I had to come up with another plan of action.

In Europe they also had a smaller golf tour for players trying to break through on to the European Tour called the Challenge Tour. It was pretty much the same thing as the Web.com Tour in America. So crazy as it all was having been a celebrity caddie on top of the golfing world not that long ago, I was now a struggling out of work caddie trying to find a job on the small money Challenge Tour. You talk about shooting yourself in the foot, fuck, I was better off shooting myself in the head.

Soon I was hanging out with a caddie called Mark who was an American guy I had first met in America. He was working for a guy on the Challenge Tour so I joined him out there getting hired by an Australian guy called Andrew Tampion. The Challenge Tour also had travelled all over Europe but the prize money was small.

Come the end of the golf season the top guys on the money list got promoted to the European Tour the following season. Working for this guy turned out to be a lot of fun but I was working on this small money tour and Pablo Larrazabal was on the European Tour making huge money playing great golf. I had honestly fucked things up so badly but that's the way it was.

This Australian guy loved to party and we had some crazy experiences travelling and working together. Most of the tournaments Tampion played rather average golf and it wasn't looking like he could get promoted to the European Tour. Come the end of the golf season the Challenge Tour had a last tournament called the Grand Final in Italy. Here only the top guys on the money list got to play and Tampion just managed to get into this tournament but he was not anywhere near the top of the money list. In fact we knew that he had to either win or come second to have any chance of getting promoted to the European Tour. The prize money at San Domenico Golf in Puglia was bigger than all the other tournaments but anything worse than second place wasn't going to get him on the European Tour.

Here we stayed in a nice hotel right on the sea and at night we hung out in small local bars and restaurants eating the best pizza in the world no doubt.

That week the golfing gods smiled on me as, come Sunday, Tampion ended the tournament tied for the lead at 5 under with a guy called Peter WhiteFord. Going into a play-off then, we knew second place was the worst outcome and he was going to get promoted to the European golf Tour for sure.

It had been a dramatic event, with gusting winds all week that had demanded concentration and adaptation from both players and caddies. As had happened in the last hole of regulation play, at the first extra hole Tampion only just failed to convert his birdie putt and Whiteford finished as champion.

Against all the odds I had found a way back onto the European Golf Tour and Tampion was over the moon to say the least. I had also made a nice amount of cash again and leaving Italy I was back on the roller-coaster. Fuck, I was like a human yo-yo, up and down all the time but somehow I always landed at all my feet. It was uncanny.

Arriving in South Africa I could relax and chill out as I waited for the European Tour to kick off in South Africa knowing I had a job again.

Twenty Four

When the new golf season arrived I went out to Malelane for the Dunhill Championship at Leopard Creek to hook up with Andrew Tampion. Meeting him, he had brought his girlfriend with him from Australia as this was the perfect opportunity for them to visit the Kruger National Park and go game watching.

The European golfers looked forward to this tournament as this setting was like no other in the world. The golf course bordered the Kruger National Park and all sorts of wild animals could be seen both on the golf course and looking over into the Kruger National Park. The guys all stayed in expensive game lodges and they ate steak all week long as here they found things cheap as they had euros and pounds to spend. They could go on game drives and it possibly was the most scenic and best golf tournament in the world simply for all these reasons.

Tourists from all over the world came here to experience this and it was a great experience for all these foreign golfers and caddies. Tampion and his lady was staying at a fancy lodge close to the Kruger Park gate and having a rental car I picked them up and drove them around.

Once the tournament got going nothing exciting happened on the golf course and come Friday, shooting level par, we missed the cut by one shot. This obviously was not a good thing but at least Andrew and his lady had time on the weekend to go do things you could only do in this part of the world.

The following week we were all off to Cape Town for the South African Open tournament at Pearl Valley in Paarl. My caddie buddy Roger had come to South Africa and we were staying and travelling together. In Cape Town we stayed in a really nice bed and breakfast and here Tampion got himself into all sorts of shit.

On the Thursday night he went into Cape Town with a South African golfer called Anton Haig who was well known for his party lifestyle, and getting totally pissed. Andrew passed out in the taxi coming back throwing up all over the place.

On Friday he was absolutely useless, hitting the ball sideways and actually making a fool of himself resulting in a ten-over 82. I wanted to laugh but it was so ridiculous that a good week had been totally spoilt.

*　　*　　*

We then had two weeks off until the next tournament, still in South Africa, so Roger stayed in South Africa and I took him with me to go visit my mother who lived in Port Edward now. I had not seen her in many years and she was an old woman by now. She lived in a retirement village in her own house and arriving there the woman had not changed at all except being a lot older. She still drank a lot and in the retirement village they had a bowling club where the old folks hung out and all these old people seem to be boozing their last days away.

Roger actually fitted right in as he was always buying all the drinks and the old folks loved him. The one thing my mother could do was still cook good food and we ate like kings. We tolerated each other during our stay but after years of having a bad relationship nothing had really changed much.

Another problem I had encountered on my return to South Africa was that my family were sick and tired of my gambling and irresponsible ways and they did not want to have much to do with me anymore. They had seen the rise and fall too many times by then and they basically had written me off. I obviously could understand this and in fact it did not blame them at all. They were totally justified as just how many times could a person fuck everything up?

*   *   *

Soon Tampion arrived back in Johannesburg for the Joburg Open tournament and, shooting one over, once again we missed the cut. After this he fired me, saying that the reason he had played badly in South Africa was that I had been giving bad yardages on the golf course. I then told him that he was full of shit and the real reason was that firstly he had played bad golf, and secondly his attitude sucked, which Cape Town had proven when he got drunk and couldn't hit the ball with a tennis racket.

So once again I was jobless and in shit with my family and things were looking bad.

Twenty Five

I knew a golfer called David Brandsdon, who I had worked for a few tournaments before, was now playing on the Asian Golf Tour and I figured Asia would be a great place to travel around. I then contacted David and he hired me to caddie for him on the Asian golf tour. I loved Asia so at least this was all going to be some fun and leaving South Africa again I was on my way to the Asian golf tour.

I met Brandsdon in Thailand as they had a tournament there and Ta was upset that I had been gone so long. During my stay things between us got really bad and she wanted to get married and have kids and I laughed telling her in that case she had to find another guy.

In Thailand my man played good to finish on the leaderboard and we were off to India next. Arriving here I discovered the biggest shit hole on God's earth. This place was a total mess and so dirty I couldn't believe my eyes. People slept on the pavements, rubbish was piled and lay around everywhere, people urinated in the streets, cows walked around shitting all over the place and the traffic was crazy with horns blaring all day long. New Delhi was a total disaster zone as far as I was concerned and I couldn't wait to get out of there. The only good thing was you could find a good curry but you had to watch what you were eating as a lot of people got the dreaded "Delhi Belly" as it was called which was a seriously upset stomach.

Leaving India I was a happy camper and going to China I was looking forward to this visit.

In Beijing we played in a big tournament that Volvo presented. Here I got to see some cool things and finding good Chinese food was obviously easy. I got to visit the Great Wall Of China and the famous Tiananmen Square and walking around I discovered markets where people all cooked and sold the weirdest things I had ever seen. One night a few of us visited a house of pleasure and they were all sorts of small pretty girls living in this place offering their services to tourists.

That week we played golf in the worst conditions I had ever experienced in rain and howling winds. My man somehow played well in these bad conditions to finish in the top fifteen making some decent money.

One night going bar crawling I lost my magic mobile phone, leaving it behind in the taxi. Everybody knew about this magic phone and it was a big loss. My brother worked for Virgin Mobile in South Africa so he had given me a cellphone but it was a pay as you go phone. When I left South Africa long before this Asian trip the phone had absolutely no credit but arriving in Europe somehow this phone kept working and it could make calls to anywhere in the world for free. It was crazy as all my caddie friends and some of the golfers always used my phone to call all over the world and it just kept on working making free calls. As I say, everybody on the golf tours knew about this magic phone, it was really amazing. Losing this phone was devastating and some lucky Chinese taxi driver had found a magic phone.

I continued to travel around Asia for a while and also a little back in Europe as Brandsdon played a few tournaments in Europe too.

In Europe I would run into my old boss Larrazabal and we were still on friendly terms and he had done very well since I had left him. These encounters always left me thinking what a dumb arse fool I had been. He was on top of the golfing world and I was always scraping the bottom of the barrel trying to survive.

In Europe Brandsdon and I finally parted company and one night in Amsterdam the same old shit happened as I lost all my money in the casino there.

* * *

I was staying on a floating barge moored on the canal and I found myself absolutely stranded in Amsterdam with no money and in serious shit. Calling my family was totally out of the question so I was now basically homeless on the streets. Thinking about my predicament I came up with a plan and I was going to go from professional caddie to "Pimp Daddy".

In Amsterdam I had spent some time in the red light district with a few girls and one of them had been a pretty girl called Roxanne from Poland. The time I spent with her we had chatted and she was really friendly and easy to talk to. That afternoon I went in search of Roxanne and finding her, I had a business proposition laid out. I told her that I could get her customers and I wanted a percentage of the money they paid her. She was happy with this arrangement so getting her mobile number I set off to put the next stage of my plan into action. I went to a small printing shop and designed a pamphlet with pictures of sexy girls in sexy lingerie offering all sorts of sexual services. I included my mobile number and said "Contact Peter", a fake name. This was now my Pimp Daddy name and I had three hundred pamphlets printed using the last of my money.

The next day I went all over town distributing these pamphlets. I first went to a lot of hotels trying to place the pamphlets in the lobbies and I had mixed reactions. At some places I got chased away and at others I managed to leave some on a table in the lobby. I handed out some to taxi drivers and I spread a lot of them around in the casino. All day I walked around Amsterdam distributing all three hundred pamphlets one way or another, even standing on street corners handing them out. Finally, late in the afternoon, I sat down at a sidewalk café to rest, ordering a beer which I could barely afford.

I honestly had not been there an hour and my phone started to ring. Answering it, a guy with a thick German or European accent asked if I could arrange two girls to do a strip show in his hotel room. Hearing this I nearly dropped the phone and I replied I would have two girls there in an hour's time. I then called Roxanne and after some discussion she said she had some friends in the business and that she would send two girls over to this guy's hotel room.

Sitting there I realised that it had all been easy enough and the next day visiting Roxanne she handed me some cash saying, "My friends were very happy, this German man paid them very well."

So there I was in the sex trade having made my first money and it was actually very funny I thought. Over the next few days I got three more calls from guys requesting girls to come to their hotel rooms. Working with Roxanne was easy as she obviously had a lot of friends in this business and she sent them to the hotels within an hour of me calling her.

The next phone call I received was the jackpot call as some guy was having a big party on one of the house boats that cruised the canals and he wanted six topless pretty girls to act as waitresses serving his guests. When he asked what the price was I took an absolute chance throwing a crazy and expensive number at him. This guy did not hesitate for a second making the deal and I knew I had just made myself a thousand euros. Soon after this I was receiving about three calls a day but some of the requests were getting crazy. One guy wanted two black girls and they had to be fat, and even Roxanne laughed telling me that she could not arrange this.

It wasn't long before I had a pocket full of cash again and this business was turning out to be a lot easier than lugging a heavy golf bag around.

By now Roxanne was not having to sit behind the window in the red light district anymore as together we were taking calls and she was sending girls all over Amsterdam, basically running things. She did go out on a few calls herself at first but this wasn't necessary once she had a good flow of girls to choose from.

One night we had some serious drama as one of the girls we sent out got beaten up by some crazy guy in his hotel room and in order to get her not to call the police we had to pay her a lot of money. In this game there was always something unexpected happening but for most part the girls got treated well by the customers and most importantly, paid well.

Roxanne and I had become good friends and business partners and she ran a tight ship employing only the best looking girls and having them tested weekly for sexual diseases. Things then got to a point where I did not have much to do as Roxanne was the captain of the ship and I spent most nights either winning or losing in the casino.

One morning Roxanne called me in a total panic saying, "Fuck, the police came to my house looking for a guy called Peter and they had one of the pamphlets you made."

Hearing this I knew the game was up then, as I honestly did not want to deal with any police that was for sure, especially in Amsterdam. I wished Roxanne well, telling her I was out of the game then and the next day I was on a flight out of Amsterdam. It had all been a crazy and fun experience and apart from banging a few hot girls I had made some good money but it was time to move on.

Twenty Six

Returning to the golf tour it was the same story as nobody would hire me for some reason, even though the Larrazabal thing was pretty much history by then. One of the caddies then suggested that I maybe go work on the Ladies' Tour. At first I laughed at this but as I had to work somewhere it was an option.

Soon I found myself in Switzerland on the Ladies European Tour looking for a job. I knew one or two ladies out there and I got hired by a Scottish girl called Lynn Kenny. I soon realized that this was a different world, as working with women's golf was a totally different ball game. This was all a big adjustment from the men's tour and it really all seemed like ping pong golf to me as these girls just kind of popped the ball around it seemed, not hitting it hard or far.

I must admit there were a few hot girls out there, but for most part they were on the average and plain Jane side with a lot of lesbians in the mix. I guess that's why people called it the "Dykes In Spikes" golf tour.

It honestly was all very boring and sedate compared to what I was used to but it was a job. Lynn Kenny was a nice fun girl but sadly during the time we were together seemed to be struggling with her game and we achieved no great results, and often we just made up the numbers out there. I worked a few tournaments in Europe on this tour but I knew I was wasting my time, also realizing that I had now worked and travelled on just about every golf tour in the world, but not being able to find a happy place again.

After this I drifted around Europe for a while returning to the European Tour and managing to work a few tournaments but with absolutely no success. By the time I finally returned to South Africa again I was dead broke, homeless and destitute. I had now fallen off this roller-coaster head first and my life was in ruins and it was all self-inflicted. Gambling had finally crippled me and I was on my own now with no more family help to bail me out.

*   *   *

Things then got so bad that I ended up on a farm near Pretoria that took in homeless people and gave them work on the farm and in return offered them a roof over their head and some food. This was all a nightmare came true as here you had the rejects of society, poor, useless and down and out people. I then got stuck in the kitchen as a chef, or rather a cook I should say, having to cook for three hundred people every day. This was like living in hell and so far removed from the world I was used to. I honestly was just about the only person with teeth in my mouth and I was living and working with the worst kind of people you could imagine.

Here I saw things I could never have imagined possible and it was all a day by day struggle to survive. Come the weekends many of the guys got drunk abusing their wives and kids and fights broke out on a regular basis. This was all the bottom of the barrel and poor kids walked around with no shoes and dirty noses and mothers sat around not really giving a shit. Being stuck in the middle of all this was really soul destroying and depressing. It was hard to believe that people could actually be like this and live this way.

I used to sit there thinking how the hell did I let things get to this point in life but I knew the answer to that question.

For a few months I endured this absolute misery until I decided that being homeless on the street had to be better than this place. One morning I woke up and, packing my bag, walked out of the gate into a blazing hot sun now homeless and on the streets. This was rock bottom and walking for miles along the road I thought ending it all was my only solution left. Crazy thoughts raced through my head and stepping out in front of a truck was the only solution I kept thinking.

I finally stuck my thumb out and later a black guy going to Johannesburg picked me up. Arriving in Johannesburg I went to a friend's house having nowhere else to go and I spent the night on the couch. The next morning my friend lent me some money and I took a bus from Johannesburg to Durban. I figured being homeless in Durban was better as the weather was warm and you could at least shower on the beach. I knew they had showers on the beach for people to get rid of the sea sand.

Things had now come full circle as I was going back to where it all had started, but broke and destitute this time. I was simply down and out. It really was unbelievable.

Arriving in Durban I had absolutely no idea what to do and I spent the first day basically walking around the beachfront aimlessly. I stood and looked at the Beach Hotel where I had worked remembering the good times I had there and now I couldn't even go and sit on the veranda and order a meal. It was honestly hard to believe the situation I found myself in and walking around I soon noticed there were many other homeless people hanging out on the beach front. I saw people digging in rubbish bins for food, others walking around begging people for money and here I was in the same fucking boat as these people.

That night, having no place to sleep, I walked around the beachfront casino finally falling asleep in a chair. The next thing I knew two security guards woke me up and proceeded to throw me out and I ended up back on the beach front walking up and down until the sun finally came up. I later went for a swim in the sea and had a shower on the beach front and I knew then I was in deep shit as I could not spend another sleepless night outside. I was also starving and spent the last little money on a loaf of bread. I was sitting on the beach front eating dry bread and drinking tap water, honestly thinking about either drowning myself or jumping off one of the tall hotel buildings. How the fuck was I going to survive out on the streets I wondered, and crazy desperate thoughts kept racing through my mind.

Walking around later I knew desperate situations call for desperate measures and somehow I had to get myself off the street as I knew I wasn't going to survive out there.

Finally speaking to a few other homeless people they told me there were shelters for homeless people and I went in search of one of these places. I then learnt that even the shelters charged a fee for the accommodation so I was back walking the streets again. Leaving the beachfront I walked up the hill towards Musgrave Centre in Durban and on my travels noticed a place providing accommodation for backpackers. Seeing this, a plan then came to mind and going to The Nomads Backpackers I spoke to the manager. I explained to him that I had been travelling around the world on the golf tours and now found myself in financial difficulty. I said that it was going to take me a few days to arrange some money as I had by then decided that I was going to ask some of my caddie buddies for help. The manager was very cool about everything telling me that I could stay in one of the dormitory rooms until I had sorted my finances out. I could see that he dealt with people always travelling and he was really very relaxed about everything, helping me out.

Finally, even if it was only temporary, I was off the street and I collapsed on a bunk bed and slept for hours.

Twenty Seven

That first night at The Backpackers I used the Internet and, using Facebook, I got hold of some of my caddie buddies. My good mate Roger I had travelled with before agreed to help me by sending me some money the next day via Western Union money transfer. The next day I collected the money and paying for the accommodation a lot of stress and strain had been taken care of and I now had to figure out what the next step in life was.

The Backpackers turned out to be a really cool place with people from different countries coming and going and for now it was home. It was also cheap and I had time to figure things out.

The place was owned by a friendly lady called Leigh who was a real free spirit and a kick back from the old hippy days. It was not uncommon to see people hanging out and smoking weed in the garden. People from all walks of life were in and out mostly young travellers and it was a free for all situation mostly. Guys and girls slept together in dormitory style rooms and privacy was non-existent. The relaxed atmosphere and cheap prices attracted many travellers and tourists who preferred this to impersonal and expensive hotels. There were always interesting people to chat to and share stories with and a great place to socialize if that is what you wanted to do.

Here I could cook food as there were two kitchens and it was really like living at home with a bunch of interesting and cool people floating in and out. I spend a few days walking back to the beachfront, hanging out, realizing just how lucky I had been to escape the streets I had been on earlier. I also knew that in the big picture only golf could ever save me but I had let things slide totally out of control and getting back there seemed completely impossible. I also knew how difficult it was to find a job out there and looking at things realistically the golf tour did not look like an option, as much as I knew it was the only thing that could put me back on my feet.

For the next few months I stayed at The Backpackers living on money my caddie buddies sent me and looking for a job but I couldn't find anything. The job market in South Africa had changed radically by then and being a white guy with mostly golf experience no doors were opening for me. I spent my time reading books and being totally unproductive and I was a lost person in this big wide world.

*   *   *

Finally the European Golf Tour returned to South Africa and the South African Open was being played in Durban of all places. Here was an opportunity to maybe find a job again and when the Tour arrived in Durban I was out there boots and all, looking for a bag. Many of the caddies were surprised to see me, asking me all sorts of questions.

I then discovered another problem, as here in South Africa the caddie thing worked a lot differently to things in Europe. Here you had all the local black caddies looking for jobs as they all knew the European golfers paid good money. These guys would fight amongst themselves and get the bags of European golfers and a white guy had no chance.

Some of the European golfers came to South Africa without caddies as they were either new pros on the Tour or because they knew they could get local black caddies for the cheaper rate. So I was looking for a bag but I had to be really careful not to clash with the black caddies and this made things a lot more difficult for me.

In Europe it was all totally different as golfers all arrived at all the tournaments with caddies and things were organized. So there, thinking about this predicament, I knew that somehow I had to be a step ahead of all the local caddies. I then found out that all the European golfers were staying at the Maharani and Elangeni hotels on the beach front so I headed over there from the golf club. I figured at least here I could talk to some golfers without having to look over my shoulder.

Walking around the hotel I then ran into a caddie from Scotland I knew and I explained my situation to him. Hearing my story he said, "Hey, I know a guy called Elliott Saltman who is coming over to play and I know he needs a caddie."

He then told me that two brothers Lloyd and Elliott Saltman from Scotland had got their European Tour cards at the Qualifying School and they both were coming to play in the South African Open in Durban. He then gave me their cell phone numbers and I immediately send these guys a text message. It didn't take long before I received a message back from Elliot Saltman and he hired me for the tournament. I actually knew his brother Lloyd from before, having met him in Europe somewhere, so against all the odds I was back working on the European Golf Tour again.

A lot of things in this world of professional caddies revolved around who you knew at times and this was one of those times. The caddies often had their own information network going on between themselves, letting each other know about open bags, who got hired and who got fired. Many guys actually picked up bags this way and it had also worked for me this time.

Twenty Eight

Going back to the golf course now I had a bag and thank God did not have to deal with shouting and fighting local caddies.

I then walked to the golf course and the next day I met Elliott Saltman at the golf course. This guy had to be the largest golfer in the world I thought as he was huge. I later learnt that he had also played rugby for Scotland and this was not hard to believe. He was a really nice guy and his brother remembered me from our meeting in Europe somewhere.

Playing the practice round Saltman asked me if I wanted to caddie for him in Europe that year, so suddenly out of the blue I had a permanent job back on the European Golf Tour. The human yo-yo had struck again as I was up and running again.

That week we missed the cut and next we were off to East London for the Africa Open tournament. I finally had some cash back in my pocket and I was back on the roller-coaster again.

At the African Open on Thursday Saltman played great golf to shoot a 67 and we found ourselves on top of the leaderboard. After my homeless experience it was great hanging out with my caddie buddies again, staying in a nice hotel and living the good life once more.

Come Friday we stood on the 17th tee box still leading the tournament, and then things changed as this guy made back to back bogies on the 17th and 18th holes. Finishing up we were however still on the leaderboard and things were looking great. That Friday night a lot of the golfers and caddies went to a beachfront pub and restaurant called Buccaneers and it was party time.

Come Saturday my man Saltman suddenly lost his putting stroke and we dropped off the leaderboard.

That night sitting in the pub one of the caddies said, "Hey, did you know that your man has been accused of cheating and he must appear before the European Tour disciplinary board about this?"

This guy went on to explain to me that back in Europe at a tournament Elliott Saltman had been called out by his playing partners for apparently marking his ball incorrectly on the greens. This was news to me and finally on the Sunday Saltman brought up this subject. He told me that he had been accused of marking his ball incorrectly back in Europe and that he had to go to Dubai to appear before a disciplinary board. As things finally unfolded later he got a three month ban from the European Golf Tour although he denied having done anything wrong.

This then meant that both he and I had to wait out the three month ban before we could get back on a golf course again.

* * *

I spent the three month period staying with my mother in Port Edward and as it went it was an up and down three months dealing with the old lady's moods and drinking. I in fact spent most of my time driving the old lady and her friends around from one bowling club to the next. These old folks played lawn bowls and then drinking afterwards nobody could drive home. Despite the always present friction with my mother it was actually funny and entertaining hanging out with these old folks and, as she did, my mother always had something good cooking in her kitchen at least.

* * *

After the three months I was off to Europe again to hook up with Saltman and it was back on the golf course. Nobody landed up on the European Tour if they couldn't played good golf but sometimes certain guys seemed to struggle, not being able to break through. As things turned out Saltman was one of these pros who had tons of potential but who knows why just couldn't get things together for four rounds of tournament golf.

We were having no success at all out on the golf tour, but back in there with my caddie buddies I obviously thanked them for all their help sending me money when I was stuck in Durban.

During my travels I passed through Amsterdam again and looking up Roxanne for old time's sake I discovered that she had a flourishing business going that I had in fact started. She explained to me that despite prostitution been legal in Amsterdam, it was strictly regulated and running things the way we had did not fall under this legal umbrella and that's why the police had looked into this. She was still operating but it was all on thin ice really and she had to be on her toes at all times.

That year I based myself in a small English town called Bagshot in England at a pub and hotel called "The Fighting Cocks". A few of the caddies stayed here in the off weeks and being close to Heathrow airport it was very convenient to fly in and out to all the tournaments in Europe. Being back on the European Tour was at this stage very frustrating as I had a bag but my man had struggled and finding a better bag was impossible. When this happens everything becomes a real grind and also very stressful. This obviously creates some tension and strain between caddie and player and it really was no fun at all. In this business the highs were very high, and the lows was very low, and that basically was the story.

*   *   *

Being a caddie hangout, "The Fighting Cocks" had all sorts of golf stuff on the walls placed there by different caddies. There were flags, photos of caddies at tournaments, newspaper clippings of caddies and all sorts of golf stuff. In fact my flag from the 18th hole after winning the French Open was on this wall too. One day I bumped into a caddie called Mike here who came from America. Swigging a few pints in the pub Mike asked me for my room key so that he could use the bathroom. I thought that was a little odd as there was a bathroom in the pub but I gave him the key anyway. When he returned a little later I noticed that he was sniffing a lot and I figured maybe he had a sinus problem or something. The next day I was flying out of Heathrow and arriving at the airport I checked my bag in and then put my Nike carry bag on the security conveyor belt as one does at airports.

When it came out the other side two police officers grabbed me by my arms saying, "You must come with us sir."

I panicked not knowing what the hell was happening and they took me into a security area. Here they swabbed my bag with a little cloth and placing the cloth in a machine one of them said, "Are there any drugs in this bag sir," and actually more out of nerves I laughed replying, "Never. Impossible."

They then proceeded to turn my bag inside out finding only my stuff in the bag. After a long ordeal they finally let me go on my way but I was shaken up as it was a hell of a scary experience. Weeks later I found out that Mike back at the Fighting Cocks had gone to my room and chopped a few lines of cocaine on the bedside table. My Nike carry bag had been under the table and a little of the powder had obviously drifted down onto my bag. I was not happy about any of this but I did know some of the caddies smoked weed and did a little cocaine on occasion. Thinking back this was a really scary experience at the time.

*   *   *

Travelling around Europe was also very expensive so not having any results on the golf course added further strain to matters and it finally all becomes a week to week struggle to survive really. Caddies around me were having success and living it up as I had done before but those days seemed destined to stay in the past for me.

Finally, the week before the Celtic Manor Wales Open tournament Saltman and I parted company and as it goes in this business he finally had a good week at this tournament making some big money with another caddie on his bag. In fact, on the par 3 17th hole, Saltman had holes in one in both the 1st and 4th rounds during the tournament which was incredible to say the least.

So yet once again I was stuck in Europe without a bag on the European Golf Tour and it was the same old story all over again. I obviously did not want to return to South Africa again and be in the homeless boat so I stayed in Bagshot in England spending my days drinking beer and hanging out in the betting shops betting on horse racing. Gambling was big in England so it was a social thing to hang out and gamble in the betting shops and really a fun thing to do. The real problem I had with this gambling thing was that I actually did win a lot of the time but I had no discipline or self-control and I never stopped when I was ahead. For some crazy reason I could not just get up and leave when I was winning and as everybody knows they will get you in the end if you carry on and on.

I did go back to the golf tour a few times but bags were hard to find and I couldn't get back on the European Tour again.

As my shit always unfolded I eventually lost all my money once again and there I was on my way back to South Africa broke once more. It was the same old story all over again and how many times had I seen this movie before.

Twenty Nine

Arriving back in South Africa I had nowhere to live so once again I found myself on a bus off to Durban and The Backpackers. This place had now become home for me in South Africa and arriving there once again I was part of the family it seemed. As it all went I stayed there for a few months once again not doing much, reading a lot and hanging out on the beach front. When my money finally ran out my caddie buddy Roger once again help me out and it was a day to day struggle for survival mostly.

By now I obviously knew that I had a serious gambling problem and I knew that I had to seek professional help and contacting my family I discussed this with them. My brother then agreed to help me and he arranged for me to go and check into a rehab clinic for addictions. He paid for me to get back to Johannesburg and he personally took me to the rehab clinic. The clinic dealt with people with drug, alcohol and gambling addictions and I was checked in there for a four week stay.

Here I got to meet some pretty sad characters addicted to drugs and alcohol mostly and the days consisted of seeing therapists and attending various lectures. I honestly hoped that I would get to leave this clinic healed of my gambling addiction but sadly that was not to be the case. In fact, during my stay there, I met a really rich guy whose family had sent him there for his alcohol problems and this guy felt sorry for me and leaving the clinic he gave me some money to help me on my way.

One would think that after a month in rehab a person would now use this money wisely to sort their life out but the very day I left the clinic I found myself back in the casino blowing this guy's money.

I then knew that this gambling addiction would stalk me all my life and for some unknown fucking reason I could not shake it off despite my stay in the rehab clinic.

Thirty

Eventually back in Durban I spend a lot of time on the Internet chatting to my caddie buddies wishing I was out on the golf tour with them. Spending time on the Internet I eventually chatted to a Spanish golfer I knew and he told me that a friend of his was going to need a caddie when the tour returned to South Africa again. This all then led to me contacting the friend, a young Spanish golfer called Jordi Garcia who evidently had done well at the European Qualifying School getting his European tour card. So as it went the European Tour had arrived back in South Africa and once again I was back on a golf course working for Jordi Garcia.

Watching this kid play golf I was a little surprised that he had done so well at the tough European Tour Qualifying School as I honestly did not think he had all the tools to make it out on the European Tour. The first few tournaments working for this kid finally proved this as he played rather average golf and I knew I wasn't going anywhere on this bag. Despite this it was a job paying me a weekly salary and arriving in Madeira Portugal a little spark finally appeared on the golf course.

This tournament was played on this island with the golf course located on the slope of the mountain so it was a tough week for caddies. The course was up and down and a tough walk and one of the caddies in fact had a heart attack and died on this golf course on the ninth hole a few years later.

Making the cut here easily enough on Saturday, the Spanish kid actually caught the leaders for a while, finally playing some good golf.

Come Sunday however, he couldn't keep things going and leaving Portugal I had at least experienced a brief glimpse of good golf.

*　　*　　*

As it went we travelled around Europe playing tournaments but nothing exciting was happening out on the golf courses. My caddie buddy Roger had by now moved to Torremolinos in Spain living in an apartment there. During our off weeks I stayed with Roger and we had great times cruising up and down the beachfront, hanging out in different tapas bars and pubs. This guy Roger could drink with the best and we often closed the bars down in the early hours of the morning.

One day, sitting on the veranda of the tapas bar on the beach front, I noticed a pretty waitress with the largest most beautiful brown eyes. She couldn't speak English very well but somehow I managed to make some conversation leaving with her telephone number. On my next visit to Torremolinos I called her and we went on a date one night. Her name was Antonia but everybody called her Toni. She was a really lively smiling fun girl and over some time we got into a relationship despite her limited English and we often had to use the translator app on our mobile phones to communicate properly. It was all pretty funny but we got on great and enjoyed fun times together. So I then had a steady girlfriend in Spain and she owned her own apartment in Torremolinos. When Roger and I went to hang out at her tapas bar we got the VIP treatment and we spent a lot of our off time there. Roger had a pretty English girlfriend and she also came over to Torremolinos often and the four of us got together whenever we had the opportunity.

Roger also enjoyed gambling but he at least could control it unlike me and we also spent a lot of time in casinos or in betting shops during our travels in Europe.

*   *   *

In America I had been skating on thin ice working there illegally and I guess I was very fortunate to have been able to see and experience the things that I did in that great country. On the European Tour I could work legally on the European Golf Tour but despite this I discovered other problems. Travelling on a South African passport presented problems of their own as I needed visas for everywhere I went and getting these visas and keeping them up to date was always a problem I had to deal with. There were times I had to make special trips in and out of South Africa just to get visas renewed and this was very costly and a huge inconvenience to say the least. There were times I missed golf tournaments as I was stuck waiting for new visas to be processed. The red tape was crazy when it came to these visas and it all was a pain in the arse to be honest.

The day I lost my passport at the airport in Spain I really ran into huge problems and for a few weeks I had to deal with a major inconvenience. I went to the South African Embassy and managed to obtain an emergency passport but it had no visas so basically all it was good for was getting me back to South Africa. I had golf tournaments I had to work in at the time so all I could do for a few weeks was take buses and trains around Europe as I couldn't fly anywhere. However even on the buses and trains the immigration officials in some countries checked passports so I was dodging bullets as far as I went.

On one bus trip the immigration officials got everybody off the bus to check passports and I actually hid under the seat obviously panicking and very nervous and lucky for me managed to go undetected.

Not being able to fly anywhere and having to travel under the radar on a bus presented all sorts of problems. I would be arriving at golf tournaments a day or two late and this caused problems with the golfer as it affected his golf schedule. After a few weeks of going through the stress dealing with this I had no choice but to return to South Africa to obtain new visas and passport.

When a person gets to travel around the world as much as I have you encounter many things and experience some really weird and crazy things. Travelling around the world may seem glamorous and fun but believe me it is really hard work and very stressful at times. Travel in general can be fun but often it can also be exhausting and difficult. The hours I spent sitting in airports waiting and killing time was certainly no fun believe me.

One of the problems is catching connecting flights with little time between flights. Two or three times during my travels my first flight was delayed resulting in me missing a connecting flight. This one time left me stranded in Poland of all places for two days. The airline paid the hotel but it was all a mess and a huge inconvenience.

Another big problem was arriving in a city you had not visited before. The taxi drivers took advantage of the situation taking you a long way around to get to your destination. Afterwards you would discover they had charged you three times the amount for the same trip as there was a far shorter way. I remember once taking the train and catching the wrong train I ended up going about a hundred miles in the wrong direction. Getting lost happened a lot and not speaking the local language added to the problems.

During a trip to India the craziest thing happened one afternoon. Here you had three wheel scooters called tuk tuks as taxis mostly and climbing in to one of these you took your life into your own hands. These drivers were nuts flying through the narrow crowded streets like mad men. This particular day we were flying down a narrow bumpy road and taking a corner right there in the middle of the road I saw three cows. The driver tried his best to swerve around the cows but hitting one of the cows at speed I went flying head first out of the tuk tuk. Hitting the ground hard and bumping my head I then discovered I had also landed in a pile of cow shit. There I sat with a huge bump developing on my head covered in cow shit. The tuk tuk was smashed up and the driver looked like he had a broken nose. I never stuck around to see anymore as I hobbled down the road looking for another taxi. I used my shirt to wipe off the cow shit and I finally arrived back at the hotel shirtless and in pain.

In Russia I had another bad taxi experience as leaving the airport the driver drove straight into the back of another taxi sending me over the front seat and into the windscreen. Then there was the time I arrived in Bangkok only to discover all my luggage had been lost. As things turned out I never saw my luggage again and had to buy everything I needed. Air Asia paid me out for the loss but it was a joke as the amount did not cover half the stuff I had lost.

Maybe the biggest problem I ever experienced was arriving in Germany and at the airport the ATM money machine swallowed my bank card. I was honestly stranded and had to beg people for taxi money to get to the hotel.

In Scotland one week after a golf tournament I met a pretty girl at the pub on the Sunday night. Monday morning early we were flying to Switzerland so all the guys pulled the plug early that night. I on the other hand got wasted going home with the Scottish lass. This all resulted in me missing the flight and not arriving at the golf course in time for work. I ended up in some big shit but I also knew I wasn't the first caddie to have done this. So as I say shit happens when one travels a lot but for most part it is a lot of fun especially visiting new places around the world.

I often wondered if I could add up all the costs for flights and hotels over the years what it would add up to. I'm almost sure you could buy a new house.

Staying mostly in hotels or bed and breakfasts, dinner most nights was had in different restaurants and after a few years you became a food critic of sorts. In China one night myself and a caddie called Mac who later sadly died on the golf course, went into a local Chinese restaurant. There was a huge hole in the middle of the table and they placed a wok here cooking your food at the table. I'm not too sure what we ordered but later digging in the wok with a chop stick Mac pulled out a whole chicken head still partly covered in feathers.

I burst out laughing seeing the look on this guy's face as he shouted "What the fuck!"

I always try to stay away from fast foods preferring to find the local hole in the wall restaurants discovering the local foods. Each country had its own special and different thing and often you came across things you had never seen before.

*　　*　　*

When the tour finally ended for the year Garcia and I had parted company after a fall out on the golf course in Italy and like so many times before I was without a job.

Thirty One

I was spending a lot of the end of season time with Toni in Spain when the golfer who had hooked me up with Garcia, a guy called Carlos Del Moral, hired me to work for him back in South Africa when the new golf season kicked off.

So when I say this world of professional golf is a roller-coaster I wasn't joking as it was all really crazy, travelling all over the world non-stop, dealing with the highs and lows of this unpredictable game. For me it had all been a run of lows since dropping the Larrazabal bag way back but I had to keep on trying. What else could I really do?

By now I had been in and out of South Africa many times and once again I arrived back in South Africa to work for Carlos Del Moral.

The first tournament was going to be played in Durban so I stayed at my old spot The Backpackers again. That week the rain came down in buckets, flooding the golf course and finally most of the par 4 holes were shortened to par 3 holes as the tee boxes were all a mud bath. The organizers tried everything to get the tournament played but it was a mess out there with all the water.

Despite all this Del Moral played good golf to finish just one shot out of a top ten place making a decent cheque for himself. This obviously help my cause as I made some cash too and next we were off to Johannesburg and Pretoria for two tournaments.

After the good result in Durban I had high hopes for the next tournaments and my buddy Roger had also come over to South Africa. In Johannesburg Roger and I spent a few evenings hanging out in

Montecasino drinking up a storm. As things then went we unbelievably missed both cuts at the Joburg Open and Tswane Open tournaments. Del Moral fired me before we left South Africa. As it goes in this business, his bad golf those two tournaments was apparently my fault and as I have said before some of these pros were just full of shit and blamed everyone and everything but themselves. I actually let this guy know that he was full of shit and he did not take too kindly to hearing this.

*　　*　　*

The night before Roger left South Africa we got wasted back at Montecasino and in a depressed state I didn't give a shit and I once again lost all my money in the casino.

Later, driving to our accommodation, Roger got pulled over in a roadblock and major shit hit the fan. He was drunk and giving the cops uphill and I had to calm things down, finally getting Roger to hand over some money to bribe these stupid arse South African police. Things in South Africa were really bad and corrupt since the new government had taken over and the fat lazy police force was on top of this list.

So the next day Roger left and travelled back to Spain and once again I was stuck in South Africa broke and jobless. I also knew that had I not been fired by Del Moral I would be on the plane off to Spain with Roger to see Toni and carry on working. Honestly, the fucking golf and gambling had both taken their toll far too many times and I was now sick and tired of fighting this losing battle.

Right then and there I decided enough was enough and I decided to go back to the rehab clinic to shake this gambling problem once and for all. I called the lady therapist that had helped me check in there before and a day later I was back in the rehab clinic with all the drug addicts and alcoholics once again.

*   *   *

I have covered an assortment of tales that reflect the problems gambling has caused throughout my life but I guess this problem was much bigger than I actually wanted to admit. Largely, it was a problem I had always tried to sweep under the carpet. Having spent some time in rehab clinics I got to learn that different people suffer with different addictions in life. Apparently all addictions fall under the same umbrella. The only difference being that gambling is not a physical addiction as are drugs and alcohol.

The major problem with a gambling addiction being that it is the most costly and devastating addiction of all. I say this as a guy addicted to alcohol can only spend so much on alcohol until he falls over or passes out. The same with a drug addiction, as you can only use so many drugs at one time. However with a gambling addiction there is no limit as you can lose everything in a short space of time and that is why I say it is the most costly addiction of all. People become addicted to different things for different reasons and who really knows why. For some reason nothing in life gave me the rush and provided the excitement that gambling did. It is hard to explain but for some reason I was controlled by some demon it seemed. The sad thing really was that I fell victim to this problem early in my life and the curse followed me all these years. It really all started the very first time I set foot in a casino. Once I discovered the roulette wheel I spent countless hours watching the wheel spin round and round. It did not take long for me to discover that I had no self-control, never being able to get up and leave when I was actually on a winning streak. Most times leaving the casino broke and depressed I knew what a fool I was but the same shit happened over and over again.

During my days living in South Africa before my golf travels I honestly just worked to support my gambling addiction. Discovering horse racing also led to further problems and when they call it the sport of kings and paupers they hit the nail on the head. This, believe me, is a mugs game but come Saturday I was at the race track throwing money away. I eventually became so besotted with this whole gambling thing that I spend hours with pen and paper trying to work out systems to get ahead of the gambling odds.

When I finally left South Africa to go to America I discovered a gamblers paradise and the problem just kept getting bigger and bigger. When I started working as a professional golf caddie I started earning big dollars and this in turn led to more gambling. Most places I went to in America had casinos, and discovering Las Vegas I was like a kid in a candy store. I visited just about every casino and sure I had my moments winning big cash but as I could never get myself to leave the casino I eventually threw it all away again.

Discovering the world of professional golf was also like gambling in many ways as you rode on a rollercoaster of birdies and bogeys, never knowing what the final outcome was going to be. It really was the same excitement and rush that gambling provided. Criss-crossing America like I did there were not many casinos or horse racing tracks that I did not visit even in that huge country. Trying to live a normal life with all this shit going on was very difficult and it was impossible to actually keep all your ducks in a row. Gambling always left me in a sort of desperate situation, chasing me from pillar to post, always having to make plans to survive. These addictions change a person's rational thinking and even their personality in many ways.

Back in South Africa I had to work regular jobs so gambling was basically limited to my income but once I got to America I was making big dollar cheques every week and then it became easy come easy go. Obviously sitting in the casino for many hours throwing back one cocktail after another did not help matters as this all added to the reckless and irresponsible behaviour. As I have mentioned before all the constant gambling led me from one situation to the next and I was always a constant lost ship drifting in rough seas.

Leaving America finally things got worse when I ended up in Europe. Here I hit the big time world of professional golf making the big bucks. So as it went, the more money I earned, the more I gambled living the life of mister big spender. The really strange thing about all this was that the gambling actually pushed me into situations that led me to the top of the golfing world. However it was gambling that would finally sink my ship and send me back to solid ground. My life was a continual ebb and flow of highs and lows until I finally hit the lowest of lows.

In my travels I had got lucky many times ending up living the high life for a while but as they say, you must never push your luck. After discovering the world of internet gambling eventually things really started getting out of control as it was all so easy with hundreds of gambling options at your fingertips. Basically all you had to do was link your bank account to a betting establishment and you could go nuts. It was actually all this that finally led to my downfall as I spent just about every night gambling online, placing huge bets on all manner of sports and horse racing. As was the case in America, it was it was easy come and easy go as I was making the big bucks at the time. Looking back at everything it is not difficult to realise just what a total fool I was but the demons had me by the balls all those years and that sadly was the way it all was.

The really hard part about all this was when I look back to the great opportunities I had in life I realise clearly just how badly my gambling addiction has fucked everything up. When I eventually ended up homeless on the street and starving I could not help thinking of all the money I had flushed down the toilet and that was the most depressing thing, and very hard to deal with.

*   *   *

I was determined to make a real effort to get this problem sorted out now and for the next month I paid special attention at the lectures and listened to the therapists. Finally leaving the clinic I hoped the gambling addiction had been taken care of and I learnt that the gambling board of all institutions had in fact paid for this stay in the rehab clinic. These stays in rehab were not cheap and amazingly the gambling board had covered my expenses. I then figured that I had donated so much money to these people that it was their turn to donate some of it back.

Leaving the clinic I now faced more problems as I was once again homeless and destitute with nowhere to go. My family ties were by then non-existent and there I was back on the streets. My caddie buddies had helped me before but I couldn't ask for any more help so I was destitute and on my own and not for the first time. I had discussed all this with the head therapist at the clinic and she suggested that I go to a homeless shelter run by church people that she could contact. So there I was going from the drug and alcohol addicts to the homeless people and what a scary and desperate situation this all was.

The homeless shelter turned out to be near the airport and arriving there it was the same situation I had found myself in when previously staying on the homeless farm. Here you had the same down and out people coming from the wrong side of the tracks and I ended up in a room crowded with old beds that were falling apart. The room was packed to capacity with people all in the same sinking boat.

Here they also gave the people jobs to do in return for the accommodation and some food which was barely enough to survive on. I was stuck on the gate as a security guard, having to open and close the gate and check the comings and goings of people. The worst part of it all was that I had to work the night shift from sunset to sunrise.

I remember the nights I stood there watching the planes taking off and landing with tears in my eyes remembering all the times I had been on one of these planes flying in and out of South Africa.

Most days we showered in cold water and it was just as bad if not worse than my stay on the homeless farm. My nights consisted of staying awake at the gate and my days were spent sleeping. I tried to keep to myself mostly but as it happened in these desperate places people were often trying to get into your business and there was always some shit happening amongst these homeless people.

It honestly was a nightmare existence all over again and I had no possible way out of there.

I wasn't exactly sure what was worse, being stuck in this place or being homeless on the streets in Durban. I spend a lot of time thinking about Toni in Spain and my caddie buddies out on the golf tour and about ending my sad and miserable life. For months I lived this day to day battle and the more I tried to figure a way out, the less answers surfaced.

Finally one morning I honestly couldn't deal with this anymore and, as I had done back at that farm, I took my bag and walked out the very same gate I had spent the past few months opening and closing.

In this homeless place they had also paid the people that were doing different jobs a very small wage so they could purchase some basic goods like soap, toothpaste, toiletries and evidently this money came from donations made to the church that ran this place. Walking out of this place I had some of this money I had saved over the months in my pocket but it was such a small amount and not even enough to buy a bus ticket to Durban, as I had decided to go to Durban again.

Walking along towards the airport I figured my best option was to take this little money and try and at least double it in the casino so I could buy a bus ticket to Durban. I knew that I did not want to gamble anymore but this was the only option open to me to try to get to Durban. As it was I couldn't get there anyway so I had to try and find a way by taking a chance in the casino near the airport. So this was not gambling as before but rather forced gambling as I had no other options at all.

Thirty Two

By the time I arrived at the casino I had walked a few miles and I realized it was now do or die for me with this small amount of money in my pocket.

After cashing in the money I had a very small stack of chips and I was sweating and shaking knowing that if I lost I was either walking or hitching a ride to Durban. I always played the numbers 5 and 8 on the roulette table and the gambling gods came to my rescue that day when after the third spin the little white ball ended up on number 8.

Leaving the casino I then had enough money for a bus ticket to Durban plus a little spending money.

Arriving back in Durban I went to The Backpacker's and knowing the manager I chatted to him. Having stayed there before he was happy to let me stay until I could get hold of some money to pay for the accommodation. I had just enough money left to buy some food to cook and that was my situation in life. Although this was a bad situation it was a million times better than being in the homeless place and I now had to find a way to survive and pay for the accommodation.

Staying at The Backpacker's I met a lady who kept the books for them and she then told me that her brother had found a job driving new imported cars from Durban Harbour to various depots and dealerships located around Durban. This lady then gave me a number to contact for a job at this company and soon I found myself on my way for an interview.

The interview really consisted of a driving test and a written exam on road and driving rules mostly. Passing these tests easily I then got hired to drive new cars that came off the ships in the Harbour to different dealerships around Durban. The pay for this job was not very good but it at least was a job and I started driving new cars. The hours were very long and we started at six o'clock in the morning and you spent all day in and out of different cars delivering them all over Durban and the surrounding area.

At night I chatted to my caddie buddies and Toni on Facebook obviously wishing that I was out there on the golf tour with them. I guess in a way I was now living a pretty normal life going to work when the ships arrived with new cars and living at The Backpacker's.

One night chatting to my buddy Roger he said that he was coming over to South Africa when the European Tour started there next season and he would try and organize me a bag for the tournaments. At the end of the day I was a professional golf caddie and working on the golf tours was always going to be what I really wanted to do so I really hoped that he could organize a bag for me.

During my stay at The Backpacker's I eventually got very friendly with the lady that kept the books and we ended up getting into a relationship. She had never been married before and had no kids and was in fact a really nice lady about the same age as I was. My long distance relationship with Toni in Spain had eventually frizzled out and I was stuck in South Africa and going back to Spain ever again did not seem possible at all.

The car driving job then turned out to be a part time job as there was only work when the ships docked with new cars and when they left it could be days before more ships arrived with new cars. Financially things then got to a point where I got behind in my rent payments and life was pretty much a struggle.

*   *   *

Finally the European Tour arrived back in South Africa and Roger arrived in Johannesburg. By then he had managed to organize me a bag for at least two of the tournaments so I took the bus to Johannesburg to hook up with my buddy Roger.

Meeting Roger he told me that Toni had been very upset by the way things had turned out but she now had a new guy in her life. It was really great hanging out with my old buddy again as we had travelled far and wide together and finally I was back on a golf course again. I guess this caddie and golf thing was a lot like gambling as you were really addicted to it and the birdies and bogeys provided the rush and excitement that gambling did.

As it always happened Roger and I spent our nights in the pubs and he loved the fact that booze was so cheap as he had euros and pounds to spend.

After the boring and struggling life I had been living, being back on the golf tour was like being in heaven and I had honestly forgotten just how exciting this world of professional golf really was. I knew I was only out there for two tournaments and I tried my best to find a steady bag again but finding these bags seem to get more difficult every year. In this business once you got out of the mix it was virtually impossible to get back again as everything basically worked in a big circle.

Obviously I was hoping that good things were at least going to happen in the two tournaments, but my run of bad luck with golf continued as we missed both cuts and my brief return to the European Tour ended on a bad note.

I worked for a golfer from Sweden that Roger had worked for before in Europe but it was no cigar and when Roger left South Africa I was once again left behind. Returning to Durban I was back in the same old half sunk boat and the future definitely did not hold any clouds with silver linings. All along I had been my own worst enemy and I was paying the price big time.

I remember my mother telling me long ago after a few drinks that she had once been to a well-known fortune teller and this old lady had told her that her eldest child would be a boy and all his life a dark cloud would follow him and I now knew what this old lady had predicted had been the truth.

Thirty Three

Back in Durban things did not improve at all and I was stuck at The Backpacker's falling behind in rental payments and the golf tours seemed to belong to another life time. I knew I had lived a crazy and interesting life bouncing up and down and I had been around the world many times experiencing all sorts of things so perhaps I had now lived all I could and pulling the plug wasn't a bad idea.

Thinking about this I tried to figure out the easiest way to go about ending it all but all the options scared the shit out of me and I wasn't sure if I actually had the balls to do it. The thought was constantly in my mind and the old fortune teller had it spot on as I was really living under a very dark cloud. I had also realized that the real reason I gambled and enjoyed the golf was that I needed a constant rush of excitement and a buzz that these things provided. As crazy as it all was I needed to live on the edge for some reason but what a disastrous situation always occurred when I fell off that thin edge. I honestly thought that maybe I had a chemical imbalance in my brain and I was surprised someone had not mentioned this at the rehab clinic. The road I had travelled in life was definitely not one travelled by a level headed sane person and I was fully aware of this fact. Nobody could self-destruct as many times as I had and it all had been totally out of control.

When a person finally realises these things, and more importantly admits them, the dark cloud becomes a lot darker.

Thinking about everything, I knew that only two things in this world could save me from pulling the plug. Firstly I had to stop gambling. That was the most important factor. Secondly, somehow, I had to find a steady bag on the European Golf Tour and make the cuts out there. This was obviously easier said than done but that was the only solution to all my problems.

By now I was sick and tired of going one step forward and then three steps backwards. At this time my caddie buddy Mark had helped me out by sending some money and I stayed in Durban waiting for the golf tour to return to South Africa again.

*   *   *

When the new golf season approached I followed the results of the European Tour Qualifying School in Spain and saw that a Swedish golfer called Pelle Edberg had played well to get his European Tour card back again. I knew this guy well and had actually worked for him in Europe two or three times previously when I was out there looking for a bag during my travels. I then sent this guy a message on Facebook and about a week later he replied explaining that he did have a caddie lined up for Europe but that I could caddie for him for the first two tournaments in South Africa as his caddie was not coming to South Africa for those tournaments.

My buddy Mark was also coming to South Africa so I arranged to meet him in Johannesburg when the European Tour arrived in South Africa. I had by now decided that I was going to get my ducks in a row and go about things in a responsible fashion and try and make an effort to get back on my feet. Going back on the golf tour I obviously hoped that my luck was going to change and there I was amongst caddies that were making big money and I was on the bones of my arse.

Being back on a golf course was like riding a bicycle to me but the golfing gods were not about to smile on me. At the South African Open this guy had it going but on Friday with three holes left to play he crashed and burned, dropping four shots in a double-bogey-par-bogey sequence and missing the cut by a single shot.

After living in some deep depression back in Durban it was at least great to be with my caddie buddies again and as it went it was bars and booze most nights. The sad part of everything was that I knew I was just back out there temporarily and I knew I was most probably never going to be a permanent fixture on the Tour again unless a miracle occurred.

By the time that Edberg left South Africa we had missed all the cuts.

*　　*　　*

Trying to get back on the golf tour I spent countless hours on the internet trying to communicate with the golfers. It was pretty much like fishing and throwing many hooks into the water hoping for a bite. Having been out there I knew a lot of people but it was still very difficult to find a bag on the tour. I always checked on guys coming from the qualifying school as often they did not have regular caddies. I also knew these guys would come and play in South Africa and the advantage I had was knowing all the different golf courses.

I managed to hook up another young Swedish golfer Joakim Lagergren for the rest of the tournaments to be played in South Africa later. I honestly was trying my utmost to get things going but I now felt like an outsider in this world that I had spent so many years in.

Finally playing the Africa Open in East London later it looked like at last something good could happen as this young Swedish kid jumped on to the leaderboard and on Sunday he played great but amazingly couldn't make a single putt all day. We then missed out on the top ten finish by just one shot but I had made a little extra cash at least.

In East London we discovered a new British pub of sorts and a good time was had here every night.

I knew by then that this kid had some game and also knew that he had nearly won in India the week before coming over to South Africa. "Just maybe," I thought, I could hang on to this bag and I tried to do the best caddie job out there possible.

I knew from my glory days with now Spanish star Pablo Larrazabal that young pros mostly needed encouragement out on the golf course, especially when things were going poorly so that was what I was focused on mostly with this guy. In East London, struggling to chip well, he had actually broken his wedge over his knee in a fit of rage and this sort of thing had to be avoided at all costs.

By the time everybody arrived in Pretoria for the Tshwane Open golf tournament things looked a little brighter I thought in general. Here my caddie buddy Thomas and I decided to go in search of a Chinese massage parlour and following the GPS System in the car we got totally lost but by total fluke really found the place we had looked up in a local newspaper. This all reminded me of my travels in Thailand before and we spent a fun two hours in the Chinese massage place. This was the fun side of travelling and working with these caddie guys as everywhere the Tour went there was fun and games happening somewhere. It obviously also reminded me just how badly I had fucked my life up and in reality I was not really a part of this travelling circus any more.

When all the tournaments in South Africa finally ended I was really sad to see my friends leave the country and I so wished that I could join them on their future travels but sadly I had not managed to line up the Swedish kid's bag for Europe. As I have mentioned many times, finding a job on this golf tour is very difficult and sometimes just impossible really.

*   *   *

With a heavy heart I then returned to Durban with no future prospects in sight and the gloom and doom returned to my life. The dark cloud was back and a week later the Swedish guy transferred the money into my account that he owed me.

Sitting in the same old Backpackers one night feeling depressed I decided, "Fuck it." I was either going to improve my miserable situation or finally go out in a ball of flames.

Jumping into a taxi I then headed for the casino, knowing full well that I was most probably heading for a disaster but as always logical thinking was not the order of the day.

About two hours later I had consumed a vast amount of alcohol and as it always happened I threw money around recklessly, acting like a complete fool. When the sun finally rose over the blue sea the next morning I woke up in a folding chair in the hotel and casino garden with a hangover from hell and absolutely empty pockets. When I then started to look for a thrown away cigarette butt on the ground to light I knew and realized then the end had finally arrived and I had pushed and pushed until I really had gone over the edge. There was just no hope for me in this world. That sadly was the bottom line. The pure and honest truth.

I was now once more homeless and dead flat broke, a lost and useless soul. Slowly walking along the beachfront I knew soon I would be scratching in the dustbins for something to eat or walking into the blue sea never to return. This is what I had turned my life into, this was my destiny and fate.

I also started wondering if any sane person would ever believe a story as crazy and tragic as my story. Yes, sad but true, that's how it all ended up for me as I write this story. I am homeless and living in shelters in Durban South Africa.

The old fortune teller knew this story long before it all played out. The dark cloud finally engulfed me and all the lights went out.

*　　*　　*

In compiling this memoir several acquaintances, caddies and players – friends one and all – have all readily forwarded their contribution to be included in the weave of Pierre's story. This is the warm recollection of caddie Mark Mazo.

A large, ceramic bowl of corn flakes fell on the floor. I hadn't seen him in over two years. At first, I wasn't even sure it was him.

"No, that can't be," I said, "Goddammit, it is him."

Still rail thin, puffing away cool style on a red Marlboro, pink shirt, collar popped. Pierre Van Achterbergh, whose surname was so difficult even he was often unable to spell it, was caddying on the European Tour, and he was on the verge of being the winning caddie

160

in the French Open, one of the most prestigious tournaments in the world.

A lot had changed since I had seen him last. He had become worn out with the Nationwide Tour. It had been two years since his last top ten finish. He seemed deflated by repeated frustration, and a few, relatively small successes of my own guiltily abashed me when I was in his company. We had known each other for two years, but we had rarely spent any time together. We cordially cadged cigarettes off each other occasionally.

His gaunt cheekbones suppressed a smile when the second shot carried a seeming ocean of a water hazard and found the green on the 72nd hole. Pablo handed him the scorecard just before plunging into the pond for a victory dive. He nearly took Pierre with him. From thousands of miles away, through the glass of a television screen, he had validated his career with the all-important second victory,

"My bru, any cunt can fluke one, but twice in this game is no dumb luck," he proclaimed over Budweiser.

Several sat around a table in a basic restaurant in Scranton, and he was the centre of attention as he was now. It was the first time I had clapped eyes on him. The tone of his voice, rising and falling softly, slightly cured by cigarettes, the words delivered in a posh Johannesburg accent stuck. Even a naif such as me could tell he had a gift for chat, that he could persuade without the benefit of logic. Four years on, instead of wood panel decor and spaghetti off paper plates, he was in the summer evening and wildflowers of the Parisian suburbs, in the splendid shadow of Versailles. He was the sun-poes. He had accomplished a lot, and, at that moment, I resolved to get back into the craft.

Six months later, we were both looking for work in Seville. Rain poured, and the rankness of wet grass clippings and the perfumed tobacco of continental cigarettes hung about the cramped clubhouse courtyard. We huddled under the eaves to stay dry. He and Pablo had split at the end of the preceding season.

"Marky Mark, what the fuck are you doing over here?"

161

"I was spinning my wheels in America, same as you were."

"So you saw me and thought, 'If he can do it, I definitely can.'"

"Pretty much."

He broke out laughing. Even when his great successes had run their course, he had his sense of humour back. It was absent those last few weeks in America before he had returned to Africa. Offhand lines of glib silliness fell flat two years before, as West Texas sunlight faded into the high desert. The vacancy in his eyes sought a horizon imperceptible to plain vision, a place and time broader, beyond the big sky above desolation dotted with mesquite and ash trees. He had a plan. It had come right, but it had unravelled. He still was able to laugh.

When neither of us had sorted a job, he invited me out in the centre of Seville. We met for a beer at a pub near the Cathedral. After the first, he asked, "Marky Mark, have you ever heard of a bocquerone?"

"What's that?"

"It's this little fish, a sardine or anchovy. It has naturally dark meat, but when it's caught, it's filleted and thrown into white vinegar to marinade. Once the meat turns white, the fish is then marinated for twenty-four hours more in olive oil and garlic. They go great with beer and a bread roll."

"I'm in."

We went into the tapas bar and had an order and another and another. The wait staff was changing over, and the server calling it quits brought over the bill. The total was a little over eight euro. Upon seeing this, Pierre shot me a look of conviction.

"Marky Mark, pay this and let's fuck off."

He wasn't going to let an error in his favour be corrected.

A month later, the schedule diverged. The "A" tour was starting up where the class players were returning from America to play the big money tournaments in Europe. Caddies without work stood little chance of getting a bag out of the lot. Our prospects weren't great. His reputation had suffered in the acrimonious split with Pablo. I was an unknown. We filled a few weeks on the Ladies' European Tour. We ultimately went down to the Challenge Tour later that summer. By October, we were in the last group Sunday at the Grand Final. He was caddying for Australian Andrew Tampion. I was working for Rhys Davies. Tampion made a few birdies and had erased our one shot lead to start the day. With three holes left to play, we were two shots back of Tampo and Peter Whiteford, who had finished and was leading in the clubhouse. On the 70th hole of the tournament, an errant drive compelled Tampo to lay up. From a tricky angle, he nearly pitched in for birdie and saved par to retain the advantage. A two shot swing on the driveable par four 17th narrowed the margin to one. Rhys burned the edge on the last and was left out of the playoff between Tampion and Whiteford, the eventual winner. Pierre nearly had a trio on his resume, and that would have restored his credibility on tour.

Five months later, Pierre had remained in South Africa after he and Tampo had split. Rhys had backed up a third place finish in Malaysia two weeks prior with a win in Morocco in his next event. Pierre was the first to send me a text message.

"Well done, money bags," it read, and the following 123 characters had to do with a loan. Perhaps it was a late charge for the road lessons in Denmark the prior August, for he had taught me, at the tender age of 31, how to drive a manual shift. We looked quite silly in that powder blue Ford Ka, abruptly stopping and stalling. Clearly, he was a good teacher. After only thirty minutes of practice, I drove the 30 km to the golf course the following day and only stalled out once I turned into the car park. However, hill starts still elude my grasp.

He was forever living on handouts. He was allergic to money. Tomorrow did not exist, and today is a cock up. Compulsive impulse gave impetus to any course of action. All plans were ill-conceived and impractical. Though diminished, he persevered to be reincarnated as an unlikely narrator to his own tale.

Whether over Carling Black Label and chicken livers, watching storm clouds gather over his motherland from an outdoor bar, or in an unassuming European inn eating simple suppers of sardines in tomato sauce and chili oil served on toast, we always can make each other laugh. The stories of his privileged childhood in Johannesburg and his start in caddying never got old. Occasionally, a fresh episode of deviance would come into the mix.

Knowing him has not been a mistake. Placing too much faith in him was.

Epilogue

Finally reaching the end of the road a person basically has lost all hope and severe depression and a feeling of despair sets in. It honestly is a feeling that is difficult to put into words. You are down and out and homeless with nothing to eat or anywhere to go. I sat staring at the sea once again trying to find the courage to swim out there and end it all once and for all. Sitting there in this state your whole life actually flashes through your mind and you wish you could turn back the clock. You remember all the good times and wonder how things had progressed to this stage of despair and disaster. Your spirit by now has been broken and you think there is nothing left to live for. You also really do know exactly why all this has happened and that is the real tough part. You feel like banging your head against a wall until it explodes wondering how you could have been such a fool. From having the world at your feet there is nothing left. For three days I walked around aimlessly in a trance of sorts trying my utmost to find the balls to end it all.

I knew an Indian waiter who worked at one of the beachfront hotels and he managed to organize me some leftover food from the hotel. I used the bathroom facilities on the beach and slept in some bushes. So once I realized I did not have the courage to end things I slowly returned to reality thinking of ways out of this situation. I had burnt all my bridges especially with my family and with most of my friends and my options were basically zero. I can assure you it is totally impossible to make something out of nothing and that is the situation I was facing and dealing with. The one thing I did know was that I had a story to tell that most people would find hard to believe as this journey in life I had been on was nothing short of crazy and out of control.

Suddenly the lights that had gone out came back on as staring at the sea I stood up shouting in to the wind, "I have to tell this fucking story".

Once I made this decision the next problem was how to accomplish this. I needed a place to stay and how the hell was I going to get my story out to the world. I then went back to Nomads Backpackers and promising them all sorts of things they gave me a bed to sleep in. I could not pay for anything but being the good people that they are they let me in as I said I would come up with a plan somehow. Using the internet they had for the guests I got busy, finally getting one of my old caddie buddies to send me a little money once again begging and pleading. Once I had finished the whole story I had absolutely no idea what to do next.

During all of this I had chatted to some people on Facebook and I had told Richard Johnson about my story. A while later his one brother Robert who I knew back in America when he came to visit his brother contacted me on Facebook asking about the story. After chatting to him and telling him that I had no idea what to do next he suggested I send him the story and he would look into it. He also said that he a friend from school that wrote books and he could maybe chat to him. Robert then send me the money to post everything to him in Wales as it was all hand written on scraps of paper. After Robert received all this we stayed in contact and finally he said that this story was definitely worth telling and that he would help me. I then had to change a few things as I was no means an author, just a crazy guy with a crazy story.

The one good thing was that doing all this kept me busy and it took me out of that boat of depression as I had something to focus on. I was not sure that this story would see the light of day but it was something to do. I can only thank Robert Johnson for all his positive input and encouragement but mostly for all his help. This guy kept me believing that there was still some roads left to travel in life and I would always be grateful for the helping hand when I was in the darkest of places stumbling around. As they say a friend in need is a friend indeed.

* * *

After all my travels and experiences around the world, having made all kinds of mistakes along the way one does learn many things, especially in my case about the game of golf and being a professional caddie.

I have mentioned previously that back in the day there were no set rules or pathway to follow towards becoming a professional caddie. Everyone on this journey seems to have found a different starting point but end up travelling on a similar path working toward the same destination. Having worked on most of the golf tours in the world, from my travels and interactions with other caddies, I have some experiential advice to give those of you reading who are aspiring to become a professional caddie.

Firstly, let me stress the point that this is a very difficult business to get into, and a hard profession once inside. Most pro golfers have already got their own caddies that travel around the world with them. Secondly, this is a highly competitive field and you have to fight it out with the sitting-on-the-side caddies who already have some mileage in terms of experience and visibility. They travel around on the tours hunting for any kind of work from one tournament to the next, with the hope they will get hired.

So in a nutshell the market for professional caddying is limited and caddie jobs are few and far between, especially for those who are still green and trying to break into this scene can leave you with more pain than gain. But don't lose hope. Given the fact that I was able to have a few lucky breaks and make a go of it, so most definitely can you. There are a few different paths one can take and I have travelled them all.

For a caddie, America is very different to other tours. It is especially difficult for guys from different countries. The red tape involved with entry is seemingly endless, especially if you are going in uninvited, and the process is plagued by all sorts of visa detail and paperwork hurdles you will need to overcome. However if you do want to caddie on the PGA Tour, and you successfully navigate the aforementioned paperwork, the best route is to go hang out on the smaller Web.com Tour. Here you stand a good chance of meeting golfers getting ready for the bigger tours who might give you your first opportunities to caddie.

Once you get going on this tour you will meet a lot of caddies and golfers and the ball is now in your hand. It is all about your ability to network and put your foot forward with the main objective of finding a good player who is on the up to graduate to the PGA, with whom you click, and they take you on with them.

Guys who follow the PGA Tour looking for a bag to grab, generally come up short. Unless you have a referral, someone who knows someone, it is pretty much a closed shop and very difficult to penetrate. By the time the PGA season starts, golfers already have their trusted caddie on their bags and the caddies themselves are guarding their turf because there are large amounts of money at stake.

I believe, and have seen, that a keen and positive person that knows their golf, making a start on the smaller Web.com Tour will always find an opening, and then it is about working your way up from there. This is the first step of moving up to the door and knocking.

Your next step in is hooking up with another caddie who you can get along with. This is a strategic alliance that helps to stretch and maintain your resilience to succeed, and with whom you can share all the many expenses you will incur on the road as you follow the Tour around wherever it leads.

On the European Tour things are not any easier, but out there at least there are more options open to you to explore. Firstly, the smaller tour called the Challenge Tour is a good place to start. This is where many up and coming golfers are playing to elevate their rankings and be seen. Many of these golfers don't have permanent caddies, so it is always possible to hook up with a young pro who is on his way to the European circuit, and who appreciates your support and decides to keep you on his bag.

The next option is probably the best option. Go and find a golfer who is intending to play the Qualifying School at the end of each year. The guys playing the Q-School all use caddies and most of these golfers do not have regular caddies with them. As Q-School sits outside of being a regular Tour tournament established caddies are absent, sitting in the shadows leaving some open space for you to step up into. Once you are on the inside here it is again a game of hope, waiting for your golfer to shine and qualify for his European Tour card, if you weather the trials of the qualifiers there is a good chance he will take you with him.

As in America, and so in Europe, it is almost impossible to just pitch up at any main event on the tour and find a free floating bag to grab.

Another good outlet of opportunity is to market yourself. You can get busy on the internet and post yourself and your caddie services on golf sites. You can also start building your own network of contacts and communicate what is happening around you with your world. The caddies' golf tour is another easy opening if you love playing golf, but not the ideal situation as far as I am concerned as it does not really bring in the big golfers who you are actually trying to reach.

There are many golf tours all over the world, but at the end of the day only two major tours really count. The PGA and the European tours.

Getting into this business is like squeezing through the eye of a needle. Therefore, when you get a chance to put your head through you need to be tight and upright. Being wise about how you work with your money to find the best travel and accommodation deals. Following the ball around involves loads of travel and as an aspiring caddie you need to have your budget on a shoe string.

Being presentable is helpful, so avoid the entertainment trap otherwise you could fall victim to the late nights and boozing that caddies are well known for. Being punctual and being able to keep time is one of the most sort after attributes. Many caddies are all too frequently shipwrecked by a night of drinking and socialising.

Before you pick up a bag, take time out for a stroll around the golf course, observe and imagine the game without a club and a ball and connect with the space around you.

Basically it all boils down to walking a narrow path, and making sure you stay on the right side of the things and people around you. The golfing community of players and caddies is actually quite small and selective. Everyone is somehow connected, and having a clean slate at all times will help you to stay in touch with the wider community. If you wreck one relationship out there, the chances are you will burn other potential opportunities that are interlinked.

Over and above all of these tips from my life on the bags, you need to keep an open mind about Lady Luck. Being lucky plays a significant part in making it and this often comes down to being in the right place at the right time. For luck to shine you need to be out there in the sun doing the legwork to make something happen out of nothing.

A lot of guys get into the business by knowing someone on the Tour or having a family connection. This is common to all things in life - not what you know but who you know.

If golf and travelling is your thing, then being a professional caddie is your ultimate dream job, but this is not an easy nut to break into and it is going to take quite some cracking and loads of persistence with patience will be required.

Being a professional caddie on the USA or European Tour is an exciting life, and there are only a few positions opened at any one time. However if this is your dream, things are always possible. You have to wake up, get out of bed and step onto the road that leads to this exciting world as I discovered. Good luck.

Open Bag

Pierre, self-confessed human yo-yo, back on Tour in South Africa in June 2016. Down but never, ever, out.

About The Author

Pierre Van Achterbergh, the eldest of five children, was born in Johannesburg during the days of apartheid. An unhappy childhood afforded little stability in life and he mostly drifted in the wind.

Following the loss of a successful restaurant business on account of an out of control gambling addiction, a series of crazy twists and turns led him from South Africa to discover the world of professional golf. As a professional golf caddie living a jet set life, travelling all over the world, he hit the big time on the European Golf Tour having become one of the best caddies in the world.

Unable to escape his gambling demons, life once again came crashing down around him, bringing a return to his home country but in a homeless position.

With a life of instability and travelling, Pierre has remained unmarried though children have come from several transitory relationships. Today Pierre remains homeless and unable to find employment.

Above all else, Pierre Van Achterbergh has earned his stripes and at heart remains a PGA and European Tour, multi-event winning, professional caddie.

Printed in Great Britain
by Amazon